# 102
# Great
# Monologues

A versatile collection of
monologues and duologues
for student actors

## Rebecca Young

MERIWETHER PUBLISHING LTD.
Colorado Springs, Colorado

**Meriwether Publishing Ltd., Publisher**
**PO Box 7710**
**Colorado Springs, CO 80933-7710**

**www.meriwether.com**

**Editor: Theodore O. Zapel**
**Assistant editor: Amy Hammelev**
**Cover design: Jan Melvin**

© Copyright MMX Meriwether Publishing Ltd.
Printed in the United States of America
First Edition

**Library of Congress Cataloging-in-Publication Data**

Young, Rebecca, 1965-
   102 great monologues : a versatile collection of monologues and duologues for student actors / by Rebecca Young. -- 1st ed.
      p. cm.
   ISBN 978-1-56608-171-9
   1. Monologues--Juvenile literature. 2. Dialogues--Juvenile literature. 3. Acting--Juvenile literature. I. Title.
   PN2080.Y655 2010
   808.82'45--dc22

                                                          2010022694

                  1    2    3          10    11    12

*This book is dedicated to Heather, Kristina, and Ashley Gritton — always follow your dreams and stay true to who you are.*

# Contents

# Introduction

*Truth is stranger than fiction, but it is because Fiction is obliged to stick to possibilities; Truth isn't.*

*— Mark Twain*

And what is stranger than a teenager's life, I ask you? Nothing! That's why I find writing monologues for middle and high school students so much fun! There's nothing they don't come across in everyday life. In fact, there's more drama in the hallways, parking lots, movie theatres, bowling alleys — pretty much anywhere there's a teenager — than you'll find on any soap opera or Hallmark movie!

*102 Great Monologues* gives tribute to the many facets that make up the typical teenage life. All the emotional ups and downs have been captured in 102 unique monologues for actors to choose from. Audiences will easily connect to the story because these monologues are more real than imagined — that's the beauty of life being stranger than fiction.

*102 Great Monologues* offers 102 opportunities for actors to find something they can relate to, dig deep with, and then jump on-stage! Each monologue is short and easy to memorize and perfect for auditions, competitions, class presentations, and more!

Remember, according to Mark Twain, only fiction is obliged to stick to the possibilities. So if you've been bit by the acting bug, give it all you've got, and explore the endless opportunities that await you. In other words, go out there and break a leg!

# Section 1
# Monologues

# 1. School Play Director
## (Girl)

1      Can you put on a stupid costume and do a totally
2  disjointed dance while singing completely off-key? I thought
3  you could! Now can you say, "I'm not even close to having
4  talent?" Of course you can't! Everyone here thinks they're a
5  super-stah! They're all vying for the lead and I don't even
6  want to give them a walk-on! But what choice do I have? I
7  don't have any people with actual talent to choose from!
8      How am I supposed to get a cast from these *outcasts?*
9  Doesn't anyone *with talent* want to act in the school play?
10  They're like a bunch of monkeys performing for a banana.
11  No self-respecting singer would be caught dead on the stage
12  with them! How am I supposed to direct a musical without
13  any singers? You think anyone would notice if I had them all
14  lip-sync their songs? Who would notice if the lead sounded
15  *exactly* like Julie Andrews? As long as the sound track
16  didn't skip, we'd be in good shape!
17      Even worse are the *attitudes.* Seriously. I've had three
18  people ask me if they get their own dressing room! Or a hair
19  and makeup guy. Are you kidding me? This isn't a
20  Hollywood production. It's a school play. They'll be lucky if
21  they get costumes, much less makeup. And they certainly
22  won't have someone to put it on for them!
23      I'm just glad I'll be off-stage where no one can see me.
24  If it weren't for me getting extra credit in drama class, I
25  wouldn't be caught dead directing this fiasco! If there's a
26  person left in the audience when this train wreck is over, I'll
27  be totally surprised!

# 2. The Guilt

(Girl)

1    I just don't get it. Why do I feel so guilty? I do everything
2    I'm supposed to. I don't drink or do drugs. Heck, I've never
3    even tried a cigarette. I don't go to wild parties and I haven't
4    even ever had a serious boyfriend. My friends think I'm some
5    kind of goody-two-shoes that doesn't know how to have fun.
6        Nobody understands that I made this promise. I know
7    you only wanted me to be safe. I know you wanted to go in
8    peace and not have to worry about me. But it's not fair,
9    Mom. No matter what I do, I feel like I'm letting you down.
10       How am I supposed to go on being a normal teenage
11   girl? I feel so guilty over everything. The clothes I wear. The
12   things I say. Even the stuff I watch on television. It's like I
13   feel you there — watching me. I don't want to disappoint
14   you.
15       It wasn't like that when you were alive. Why can't I stop
16   thinking that you're looking down at me and shaking your
17   head, wishing you were here to tell me what to do ... and
18   what not to do?
19       These were supposed to be our rocky years. You know,
20   the ones when all mothers and daughters fight and hate
21   each other. You were supposed to be *here* to argue with me.
22   To ground me. To tell me, "No! You can't go to that party!
23   Are you out of your mind?"
24       It's not right that I have to be my own mother! It's not
25   right that I can't get mad at you like the other girls get to!
26   I don't get to slam my door. Talk bad about you to my
27   friends. Sneak out of my window. I don't get to do *any* of
28   that!

1    *(Pause)* I miss you, Mom. And I know you trust me.
2    That's why tonight I'm going to that party I was invited to.
3    And I'm going to make good choices. You'll see. I'm going
4    to make you proud, Mom. I promise.

# 3. Hairy Mary
## (Girl)

1     I can't remember the last time I wore a short-sleeved
2  shirt. Or how many times I've said things like, "I'm just
3  cold-blooded" when it's ninety degrees outside and I'm
4  covered up like a nun or something. I'm sure people think
5  I'm weird. Some kind of prude who doesn't want to show
6  any skin. Truth is I can't, because if I did, then people would
7  really start talking.

8     See, I've got this problem. I'm hairy. I'm not talking
9  normal hair either. I'm talking pass-for-a-bear hairy. And not
10  just the normal spots like underarms and legs. My whole
11  body is hairy. My arms. My ankles. A patch on my stomach.
12  A spot on my lower back.

13     It's disgusting to me, so why would I ever expect
14  someone else to not be grossed out by it! Still, I wish I could
15  tell someone. Someone I could trust. I keep thinking one
16  day someone will notice. One person will come along who
17  won't accept my lame excuse for wearing long sleeves all
18  year and I'll be caught. Forced to tell my dirty secret. Part
19  of me actually wants someone to care enough to delve
20  deeper. Find out why I never go swimming or dress out for
21  gym. But I guess it's easier to believe that I'm defiant or a
22  loner, or "that weird girl that dresses like a nun" than to
23  actually spend some time finding out the truth.

24     To be honest, I don't know what I'd say anyway. My
25  father was a grizzly bear? *(Laughs.)* Or maybe I could say I'm
26  part of a science experiment? That my parents signed me
27  up when I was a baby and I can't get out of it.

28     Wait! I think I've got it! I'll just tell everyone I'm actually

1    a wolf! With those new vampire and wolf books out, and
2    everyone going crazy over them, someone might actually
3    believe me!

# 4. Pantyhose Rebellion Backfires

(Girl)

1     Last year I had the worst summer job ever. Lifeguard. It
2 sounded good — hanging out at the pool all day, checking
3 out hot guys. But it was horrible. It was so stinking hot and
4 we barely ever got to get in the water. All I did was sit and
5 fry in a chair and try to keep my eyes on a zillion splashing
6 kids who must've been deaf because no one seemed to hear
7 me when I blew the whistle.

8     So I knew that was not going to be my dream job this
9 summer! Instead, I snagged a job at the bra and panty
10 store. Pretty cool because I get discounts on all the latest
11 stuff. I must own a hundred pairs of panties now. Best part
12 is there are no screaming kids *and* there *is* air conditioning.
13 I don't even break a sweat.

14     But I should've known that no job is perfect. They have
15 a dress code. Because the store sells pantyhose, every clerk
16 has to wear them — probably why no guys work here!
17 *(Laughs.)* I haven't worn pantyhose since I was three. And
18 those were tights, not hose! Don't they know that this
19 generation does *not* wear hose. They don't work with flip-
20 flops, which of course was rule number two: no flip-flops. I
21 almost quit before I'd even started.

22     Well I was determined not to wear the full-fledged, up-to-
23 my-neck, grandma-style hose so I bought a pair of thigh
24 highs. They weren't that bad ... at first. Then they started
25 creeping down my leg. I guess my thighs just weren't big
26 enough to hold them up. I tugged at the hose with every
27 step. Pretty soon the thigh highs were at my knees. I had to
28 do something.

1    I ran in the dressing room and pulled a rubber band to
2  the top of each leg. Within minutes, my thighs were stinging
3  so bad I knew that I was losing circulation. Back to the
4  dressing room. I replaced the rubber bands with little silk
5  ribbons they use to tie up the fancy pajama sets. Ahhhh ...
6  relief. They felt so much better than the rubber bands.
7    I thought I was in the clear. So I began waiting on a
8  customer. That's when it happened. As I walked over to a
9  display, *both* my thigh highs *and* the ribbons fell to the floor
10 at my ankles. As I ran back to the dressing room, I heard
11 the customer say, "Well I don't want any of *those!*"

# 5. Pick Her Upper
(Guy)

1    The show I love is coming to town and I'm getting on it!
2    I don't care what I have to do — I have got to get them to
3    pick me. It's my last hope of ever getting a girl to date me.
4    You think I'm kidding? OK, maybe you're looking at me right
5    now and you know without a *doubt* that I'm *not* kidding. I
6    haven't had a chance with a girl my whole entire life!

7    But this show, this wonderful new show, promises to
8    take loser guys like me and turn them into cool guys that
9    girls actually *want* to date! Do you know how much I need
10   a girl to *want* to date me? The only girl that even remotely
11   considered going out with me was my twice-removed cousin
12   whose date had just dumped her an hour before prom. But
13   then when I showed up, she was all of a sudden violently ill
14   and couldn't go. A coincidence? I think not!

15   But this show is going to change everything! These
16   awesome guys are going to teach me how to talk to a girl.
17   How to ask one out. What to say — or more importantly
18   what *not* to say! They say that no one has ever left the show
19   without achieving a first and *second* date! In fact, they
20   guarantee one hundred percent that you'll be able to pick up
21   chicks when you complete their program.

22   Well, let's go! Sign me up! I don't care if I have to camp
23   out for a week to get in line. I'm going to be the first one
24   there. I have to be. My mom has been getting quotes on
25   turning the basement into an apartment for me. I heard her
26   tell a friend that at the rate I'm going, which is about zero
27   miles per hour, she's pretty sure I'll be living with her
28   forever. I don't want to be that creepy man on TV that's forty

1   years old and living in his parents' basement! Someone's
2   gotta help me!

# 6. Confused at 17

(Guy)

1     So I'm supposed to know exactly what I want to do for
2  the rest of my life — the whole fifty-something years until I
3  get to retire — right now?! At seventeen?! I *barely* know
4  what I want to eat for lunch! I *barely* know whether I prefer
5  boxers or briefs! I *barely* know if I want cheese on my burger
6  or not! How can they expect me to choose a career?
7     I can't even settle on a college! But duh, that's because
8  I can't settle on a career. This college is good for this. This
9  college is good for that. You have to go *here* if you want to
10  do *this*. Blah, blah, blah! Don't they have any colleges that
11  are good for not specializing in *anything*? Because *that's*
12  where I want to go. The undecided school! A place that
13  doesn't put you on the fast track to a lifelong career. I want
14  to take my time. A school that you can mosey along
15  through. Try out different things. See what you like. A
16  school with *no* expectations! That's what I want.
17     I mean, I'm going to have to do this thing, this career,
18  for the rest of my life! Shouldn't I be absolutely *sure* about
19  it? I don't want to be like my parents. They look like two
20  zombies. Going to work every day, eyes glazed over like two
21  robots on autopilot. I want to *love* my job. Is that too much
22  to ask?
23     So you people get off my back. When I know what I want
24  to be, I'll let you know. For now, just sign me up for knitting
25  one-oh-one. I hear it's a great way to think!

# 7. Can't Anyone Take a Joke around Here?
## (Guy)

1     Why is it that I can say things that absolutely no one
2 ever hears — or listens to — but I say one smart-aleck thing
3 about my car and now I'm walking? I wasn't trying to be
4 ungrateful. I know my parents aren't rich. I *know* they didn't
5 *have* to buy me a car. I *know* they provide a roof over my
6 head ... and food on the table ... and pay my sports fees ...
7 and blah, blah, blah. I *know* all of those things. But can I
8 help it that when I saw the "duct tape mobile" I wasn't
9 exactly overjoyed?
10     The car looks like it came straight from the junkyard. I
11 was shocked the thing actually had an engine in it! The fact
12 that it was running was near impossible. The muffler, the
13 bumper, and the right front fender — oh, and the left mirror
14 — were all being held on by duct tape! I'm not kidding. Is
15 that even legal? Can you drive a car that might lose its parts
16 driving down the highway?
17     But I didn't mean it when I mumbled that I'd rather
18 walk. It was a joke ... well, a semi-joke. I'm sure as soon
19 as I got used to the car I would've been more of a sport
20 about it. The initial shock was just too much to bear. Even
21 the best actor in the world could not have acted excited
22 about that thing. I'm only human! A teenage boy with
23 visions of sports cars and spinners on his wheels. And a
24 bumpin' stereo. I'm pretty sure that contraption still had an
25 eight-track player. Maybe I could dig out Mom's old Barry
26 Manilow tapes and go for a spin. Oh, there I go again! I can't
27 help it. The Duct Tape Mobile just gets to me.
28     The Duct Tape Mobile ... it sounds kind of cool, doesn't

1    it? Maybe it won't be so bad after all. It'll be kind of retro. I
2    can fix it up ... that is, if they'll even give it to me now. I
3    can't believe this. I'm actually going to have to *beg* for them
4    to give me that car! I just wish I'd put some of that duct
5    tape on my mouth!

# 8. Two Garbage Cans, a Mailbox, and a Cat
### (Guy)

1    It all started a few weeks ago when I went to take my
2  driver's test. Everyone in school had already been making
3  fun of me and my bad driving just because my bigmouth
4  brother told them about me hitting two garbage cans, a
5  mailbox, and a very unfortunate cat. It sounds worse than it
6  really was. They were all at the same time; it's not like I had
7  three separate accidents! But that's one of the joys of going
8  to high school with an older brother. He likes to run his fat
9  mouth and tell embarrassing stories about me.

10  So of course I couldn't fail the test. Everyone was
11  expecting it. Told me I was going to get a score so low they
12  would probably make me give back my permit. Yeah. They
13  were real funny. I couldn't give them the satisfaction of
14  being right. No wonder I was so nervous. Who could drive
15  well in those conditions? All that pressure?

16  I flunked. Bad. So I lied. Told everyone I aced the test.
17  Told them the officer said I was the best driver he'd ever
18  seen. They figured I was exaggerating a little. But they
19  didn't figure that I out-and-out lied. Not even my brother. I
20  swore my mom to secrecy.

21  Now everyone keeps asking me for a ride home from
22  school. My brother, in what can only be described as a weak
23  moment, even offered for me to drive his car home when he
24  had to stay late. Said I could come back and get him.
25  *(Pause)* I *almost* did it. Who would know, anyway? But then
26  I thought about the crumpled trash cans, bent over mailbox,
27  and buried cat. There was no way I was taking that kind of
28  chance. All I know is, this week I have got to *pass* that test!

# 9. Road Rage Victim
## (Girl)

1   There I was, minding my own business, singing to my
2   radio like I always do, when I look in my rearview mirror and
3   this woman is obviously waving her hands and yelling at me.
4   I can't tell what she's saying, but I know it's not good. I look
5   back at the light in front of me, hoping it turns green soon
6   because I can't wait to get away from her.
7       So that's where my mind is: focused on the light. Then
8   all of a sudden the woman is at my window!
9       I guess I'm in shock, because, not even thinking, I
10  actually roll the window down about halfway to see what she
11  wants. That's when she reaches in to pull my hair with one
12  hand and slap me with her other one! "You cut me off!"
13  she's screaming. It's all happening so fast. I try to pry her
14  hand out of my hair and block my face at the same time.
15  "Who do you think you are? Cussing *me* out?" she says.
16      Me? When did I say anything to the woman? I've never
17  seen her before in my life, and if I did cut her off, I certainly
18  hadn't meant to! I'm a new driver — only sixteen. Maybe I
19  made a mistake ... I'm trying to process what she's saying
20  while forcing myself to react to her hitting me. Finally, my
21  brain kicks in and I pull the button to put up the window.
22  She has no choice but to get back or lose her arms. The
23  light turns green and I hit the gas, speeding through the
24  intersection. My hands are shaking so badly I can barely
25  drive, but there's no way I'm stopping in case psycho
26  woman decides to come after me. Of course I watch my
27  rearview mirror the entire time.
28      Ten minutes later there's still no sign of her. I pull into

1    a gas station parking space and burst into tears. I relive the
2    attack over and over in my head and I finally realize why the
3    woman thought I was cussing at her. She saw me singing
4    and because she was yelling things at me, she thought I was
5    yelling things back at her. My brother always warned me
6    that my singing would get me into trouble, but I never
7    thought it would be anything like this!

# 10. Uncle Creepy

(Guy)

1     OK, so I wasn't exactly thrilled when the will was read
2  and there was no one but *me* to take care of the little brats.
3  Yes, I admit it, I didn't always think of my sister's children
4  as fondly as I do now. But what can you expect? I'm barely
5  out of high school. A bachelor, thrust into the throes of
6  parenthood. Who would've dreamed that I'd be their closest
7  living relative?

8     But it didn't take long for me to see how precious the
9  little boogers are. I know I have a strange way of showing
10 affection, but not every family thrives on hugs and kisses.

11    Now Social Services says I'm not providing a good home
12 for them. It's an outrage, really, these accusations! Saying
13 I'm taking their money. How can they say this about me?
14 Look how much I've spent on them since I started caring for
15 them. I've had to work two jobs! They don't think about the
16 food and clothing I've provided. Not to mention a roof over
17 their heads. My entire paycheck goes to caring for them and
18 I've yet to be thanked for any of it.

19    I'm not asking for compensation. I only want to help
20 *manage* their inheritance so that they can have even more.
21 I don't make that much money and can't provide them with
22 the luxuries they deserve. Why, if I could get my hands on
23 just a bit of their inheritance, I'd buy the sharpest silver
24 convertible Lamborghini with white-wall tires and black
25 leather interior ... *(Acts lost in the thought of it all)* for them,
26 of course! You see, I only have their best interests at heart.
27 Just think how cool they'd look riding around in a car like
28 that! They'd be the envy of the school. Instant popularity.

1   Now if that doesn't sound like a devoted uncle, I don't know
2   what does!

# 11. The Ghost of Fred Astaire

## (Guy)

1    Never in my life, or death, have I seen such an outrage!
2    Young men manhandling a woman like a piece of meat.
3    *(Points.)* Look at the way that boy is groping that young girl.
4    Like he owns her. And all that bumping and grinding. A girl
5    could lose her innocence out there.

6    Someone needs to teach these boys some respect.
7    Show them how to treat a lady. How to dance with grace
8    and dignity instead of vulgarity! They're acting like a bunch
9    of animals out there. How can anyone even call that
10   dancing? It's obscene. Like something from a dirty old
11   movie. They've taken the romance out of the dance. Where
12   is the grace of twirling a woman around the floor with
13   dignity? The fluid movements? The synchronization of two
14   bodies moving to a gentle rhythm?

15   The music is so loud and pounding, it's no wonder they
16   can't truly feel it. There are arms and legs and other body
17   parts flying around in abandonment! That's not dancing! It's
18   craziness. And the few words I can actually understand are
19   completely inappropriate. *(Pause)* Did you hear that? More
20   swear words than a ship full of drunken sailors! And they're
21   dancing to it! No wonder they've lost all sense of propriety.
22   The songs are practically telling them what to do.

23   Oh, how I miss the days of graceful dancing. Holding a
24   woman in your arms like something to be treasured.
25   Touched delicately as if she could break like blown glass or
26   a fresh flower.

27   *(Pause)* Not that I wouldn't have minded a little close
28   dancing with Ginger Rogers, mind you. Now she was one hot

1   babe! But that woman would've slapped my face if I tried to
2   put my hand anywhere close to where these guys are
3   touching. Yes sir! That woman was a lady.

# 12. The Hero

(Guy)

1    Hi! My name is Josh Brown and I am the hero of Scott
2    County High School. Everyone knows who I am. Some might
3    even say I'm a legend.
4        You probably think I've done something heroic. Saved
5    someone's life. Or maybe you think I'm some sort of sports
6    superstar. Scored the winning point at State or something.
7    But that's the farthest thing from the truth! I haven't done
8    any of those things.
9        What I did was something every guy dreams of doing: I
10   dated sisters. *At the same time!*
11       It's true! While dating Rose, I asked her younger sister,
12   June, to F.R.O.M. That's the freshman version of prom. So
13   one week I was at F.R.O.M. with June and the next week,
14   prom with Rose. It was awesome!
15       Truth is, I didn't start out to date them at the same
16   time. I was perfectly content to only date Rose. But then I've
17   had this thing going since I was a freshman: I wanted to be
18   the only one in school that went all four years to F.R.O.M.
19   You can only go if you're a freshman or you're the date of a
20   freshman. I couldn't let a little thing like dating a non-
21   freshman get in my way!
22       So now you're probably thinking, "Big deal. So he did a
23   pity date for his girlfriend's sister who couldn't get a date
24   *and* he got to hit his four-year goal." Not true! Not true at
25   all! June is *hot!* Smokin' hot! She turned down three other
26   guys to go with me. If anything, *she* took pity on me! Either
27   that or she has some serious issues with her sister, but we
28   won't go into that.

1    I had a blast on both dates. Trouble was, it couldn't last.
2    Rose broke up with me ... *after* prom, of course! But can you
3    blame her? Come on! I dated her sister!
4    But I don't care. It was completely worth it. Not every
5    guy in high school gets a shot at being a legend!

# 13. Wanna Go ... Talking?
## (Guy)

1   Truth is, we were parking. The story I told the truck
2   driver, the Volvo driver, the cops, the tow truck driver, and
3   my parents — we were talking. Someplace private because
4   we were fighting and then we got stuck turning around. How
5   many of those mentioned actually believed my story? None.
6   Although my parents were actually swallowing it hook, line,
7   and sinker until the cop pointed out that we'd crushed part
8   of a crop when we came out from being parked *behind* the
9   barn.
10   Here's what happened: My girlfriend and I *had* been
11   fighting. Over something stupid that doesn't even matter
12   anymore — like I didn't call her or something. But we'd
13   made up and wanted a little make up make-out session.
14   Only both our parents were home. We decided to take a
15   drive out to the country.
16   I found the perfect spot right off the road behind a
17   dilapidated old barn. Clearly no one used it. So we had our
18   make-out session until the clock on the dashboard said it
19   was past time to get home without facing getting grounded
20   for life.
21   The windows were all steamed up from all that "talking."
22   I thought I could see through them. *(Mimics.)* "J.R., you'd
23   better wipe those off, or you're going to hit something!" my
24   girlfriend said, which of course made me that much more
25   determined to drive as they were.
26   Well, good news is, I didn't hit anything. I drove us
27   straight into the biggest ditch known to man. Seriously, my
28   car was practically vertical in the air! Our heads even hit the

1   windshield when the thing tilted.

2      Along came a man in a truck. One chain and a detached
3   bumper later — his bumper, by the way — still stuck. Along
4   came a Volvo. "I'll call the police," the woman yelled as she
5   waved and drove by. Along came the police … and then the
6   tow truck … and *then* my parents. It was definitely *not* the
7   way one wants to end a steamy make up make-out session.

8      The good news is, my girlfriend is mad at me for not
9   listening to her about the steamed up windows. So, when
10  I'm not grounded any more, I'm pretty sure a good apology
11  and a lot of groveling and I'm guaranteed another make up
12  make-out session! And this time, we're staying in the city!

# 14. Worthless Father

(Guy)

1     So I guess they don't have pens in prison. I mean, that
2  would explain it, right? 'Cause why else would a man choose
3  to ignore his one and only son? It's been like six months
4  since I wrote him — my dad. I don't even know why I did it.
5  I mean, come on, what was I thinking? What did I expect?
6  An apology?

7     Why do I even let it bother me? He's not worth it. He's
8  not. He's just a psycho that deserves to rot in jail. I
9  shouldn't even *want* to talk to him. What could he possibly
10  say? "Uh, sorry I tried to run over your mother, son, but she
11  was really getting on my last nerve. I didn't do it to hurt you.
12  I still love you. You have to believe that ... "

13     I mean seriously! What was I expecting? *(Pause)* Well, I
14  guess I was expecting something ... anything ... not silence.
15  Not rejection. Not again. I mean *who* is *he* to reject me? To
16  turn his back on me as if he doesn't even know me! Even
17  after everything he's done. Even after I gave him this
18  chance!

19     *(Pause)* I have this friend. He tries to understand. He
20  says he knows what I'm going through. But what could Jake
21  possibly know about this kind of betrayal? How could he
22  possibly understand what it's like? I've never felt so alone.
23  Dad didn't just take my mom, he took my life.

# 15. Kindergarten Tragedy

(Girl)

1     Hi, my name is Angela. My mom used to call me Angel.
2    Used to. A long time ago. *(Pause)* I was at school.
3    Kindergarten. I remember standing there. Backpack on.
4    Expecting at any moment for her to pull up, apologize to the
5    teacher, and then speed off with me safely buckled inside. I
6    wasn't even worried. Not at first. I mean she was a few
7    minutes late every day. I don't even think the teacher was
8    worried. Mom definitely wasn't the most punctual person in
9    the world. Most mornings I came to class in the middle of
10   the pledge. I was destined to a lifetime of report cards with
11   numerous tardies. That was life.
12    Anyway, I guess it wasn't until the teacher, Mrs.
13   Carpenter was her name, told me that maybe we should wait
14   inside. I guess maybe that's when I knew something was
15   wrong. But it might have been a few minutes earlier because
16   I remember my backpack was starting to feel heavy on my
17   shoulders and I'd never remembered that heavy feeling
18   before.
19    So we moved inside and waited. My teacher waited with
20   me, at first. But as it got later and later, she had to leave.
21   She had her own kids she had to get home to. Calls were
22   made. Whispers and stares. The principal, the secretary,
23   and even the custodian looked at me with faces that told me
24   something was very, very wrong.
25    I started to cry. Probably not knowing what else to do,
26   they bought me a soda from the vending machine and told
27   me everything was going to be OK. I remember thinking that
28   Mom wouldn't like me drinking it. Soda was for special

1  occasions only. Like at the movies or when Mom sold a
2  house.
3      But I drank it anyway. Feeling guilty. Feeling worried. It's
4  funny, but later I remember wondering if maybe God had
5  punished me for drinking that soda. Because I knew I
6  shouldn't have but I drank it anyway.
7      It wasn't long after when the police came. They talked to
8  the principal and then they talked to me. They told me that
9  she wouldn't be coming to get me. They told me about my
10 mother being in a car accident not far from my home. They
11 told me that my mother was dead.
12     It was hard for me to understand. She wasn't just late.
13 She hadn't forgotten me. She was dead. Just like that. You
14 know what? That was seven years ago and I haven't had a
15 soda since.

# 16. The Magnet Man

(Guy)

1    Let me tell you, being a superhero isn't all it's cracked
2  up to be. Do you know how sick I am of picking nails out of
3  my butt? Or staples? Or paperclips? Or anything else metal
4  that people just casually leave lying around? I can't even
5  think about walking near a construction site! It'd be like
6  committing suicide. I have to go three blocks out of my way
7  just to go to the grocery store.
8    Then I can only go down a couple of aisles. Forget the
9  canned goods. It's fresh veggies only. No big deal, they're
10  healthier, right? But I sure would love a good old can of
11  baked beans every now and then!
12    Of course the kitchen isn't any picnic either. Do you
13  know how hard it is to cut a steak with a plastic knife?
14  Especially since I have to cook the darn thing in the
15  microwave. No oven for me — too much metal! The steak is
16  pure rubber. I go through more knives than I do toothpicks!
17    Thank goodness TV dinners have come a long way. I'd
18  be starving to death if it weren't for premade meals. Well,
19  that and delivery. I just have to make sure the delivery guy
20  isn't packing any change, otherwise, it's pepperoni pizza
21  with an extra hard crunch! I've had more silver in my mouth
22  than a kid in braces.
23    Why couldn't I have gotten more normal super powers,
24  like flying or being invisible? Something cool and not life-
25  threatening! Why would anyone want to be a magnet? A
26  human attractor of every sharp and pointed thing imagined?
27  Well, there is really only one magnet I'd ever *want* to be —
28  a *chick magnet* — oh yeah! Sign me up for *that* superpower!

# 17. Fuzzy Wuzzy

## (Guy)

1     Have you ever had a really great idea? You know the kind
2  — this-is-going-to-change-my-life kind of idea. And then you
3  just run with it and this thing that you thought was going to
4  make your life so much better just made your life stink that
5  much more?

6     Well that's what happened to me. *(Holds up permanent*
7  *marker.)* See this? An ordinary permanent marker. Or as I
8  like to call it, "The pen that made me the laughing stock of
9  the entire school."

10    Yeah, I know it's not the pen's fault that I'm a complete
11 and utter moron. No, that would be the fact that I came up
12 with this brilliant idea at three in the morning. Let me make
13 this clear: *no idea* is good when you come up with it at three
14 in the morning! Brains just don't function well at that time.

15    Obviously. *(Points to chin.)* See this? This is a three a.m.,
16 change-your-life decision gone bad. "What is it?" you ask.
17 Well, if you can't tell, which apparently *no one can,* it's a
18 goatee. A lame excuse of a goatee for a guy who can't seem
19 to grow anything other than what looks like *lint* on his chin
20 and upper lip!

21    So I darkened it in a little. Thought it might make it look
22 thicker, the way normal face hair looks. But now I just look
23 like a clown and it won't wash off!

24    It's so unfair. I'm twelve years old! Every guy has face
25 hair by now! Where's the real mustache and beard? Where's
26 the five o'clock shadow? The deep, sexy voice? Where's the
27 growth spurt to six feet tall? I've been genetically gypped!
28 How am I supposed to survive in a school next to cavemen-

1    looking guys who have more hair in their ears than I have on
2    my face? I might as well write a big L on my forehead. *(Acts*
3    *like really doing this. Pause. Realizes what he's done.)* **Oh man!**
4    **I gotta go find some soap! Or bleach! Or maybe some acid!**

# 18. Good Ol' Tom
## (Girl)

1     My friend Lisa and I have been friends since
2  kindergarten. We do everything together. When we were in
3  middle school we started this coded language for those
4  *special* times of the month. It just made it easier to talk
5  about female things without anyone else knowing. So there
6  we were standing at my locker talking about how "Tom"
7  came to visit me over the weekend. And guess who heard?
8  My boyfriend, of course. Now he's all mad and jealous and
9  is demanding to know who the heck Tom is. I'm not about
10 to tell him that Tom is that "magical" time of the month that
11 all girls dread. Get it? *T-o-m? Time of month.*
12    So now I don't know what to do. I can't tell him what
13 Tom stands for. That's just not something I want to share
14 with a guy, even if he is my boyfriend. The last thing he
15 needs to know is my cycle! Then he'll think he has me all
16 figured out and be like, "Ohhhh, so that's why you were
17 grumpy this weekend," and stuff like that. Or when I pig out
18 on chocolate he'll look at me all-knowing like he's figured
19 out everything there is to know about the female body!
20    I rushed off to class before he could say too much, but I
21 know he's mad. I guess I can't blame him. He thinks I'm
22 cheating on him. Somehow I've got to come up with a
23 believable fake person named Tom who would've come to
24 visit me this past weekend. Someone who won't make
25 Jason jealous. Someone that was so unimportant I forgot to
26 mention that he was even coming. Someone he'll never, ever
27 expect to meet.
28    *(Pause)* I've got it! Tom can be my distant cousin. The

1    son of my Aunt Flo! Get it? Aunt Flo? Oh, that'll be
2    hilarious!

# 19. Leaves of Three
## (Guy)

1　You know how you can look back at something and you
2　can pinpoint the exact moment that things started going
3　wrong? And you know without a doubt *what* caused that
4　horrible shift from a good day to a bad one? Well, I can tell
5　you exactly what it was. Potato salad. In and of itself, not
6　necessarily a bad thing. But I should've known something by
7　the yellowing color of the mayonnaise. Common sense did
8　not prevail. It smelled OK. It tasted OK. But I can say with
9　one hundred percent certainty that the potato salad I
10　scarfed down for lunch was *not* OK. But that was just the
11　beginning.

12　We were over an hour into our hike when the cramps
13　started. Then came the sweats. In ninety-degree heat that's
14　not such a big sign. But *then* came the chills. That's when
15　I knew things were going to get rough. The second set of
16　cramps came fast. I had no choice but to find a tree.

17　Have I mentioned yet that I'm not a camper? Not a hiker.
18　Not a fisherman. Not a hunter. In fact, I've barely spent a
19　day outside in my whole life. I'm a computer geek, pure and
20　simple. A bathroom for me is never more than a room away.
21　But not today. Today I had been suckered into helping a
22　friend of mine earn a badge by leading a bunch of little kids
23　on a hike. To be honest, I was the poster boy for his whole
24　this-is-what-you-should-never-do speech. I was OK with that.

25　But back to the tree. Given the fact that I have never
26　actually found a tree for that purpose, I wasn't exactly clear
27　on how that would work. I understood the hiding behind it,
28　but that's about the extent of it.

1     "Grab some leaves," Andy said.

2     "Don't be such a girl," the little punk hikers said.

3     And that's where the second moment of disaster came
4 in. No one said anything about what type of leaves to use.
5 No one thought to mention the annoying chant about
6 "leaves of three." Oh no. No one breathed a word about
7 being careful in your fake toilet paper selection. At least not
8 until later. That glorious time later sitting around the
9 campfire when I realized that I hadn't sat on a pile of ants.
10 That wonderful crawly itchy feeling was the outcome of
11 using *poison ivy* as nature's toilet paper!

12     Just in case you were wondering, this was officially my
13 first and last hike.

# 20. Whoa, Baby!

## (Guy)

1     Graduating from eighth grade is a great time in every
2 person's life. At least it's supposed to be, right? A whole
3 new world opening up. The world of high school. The world
4 of getting older, getting a license, dating, parties, and so
5 much more! So of course I was excited about the prospect.
6 Even pretended I didn't have a clue about my mother
7 inviting the whole basketball team over for a surprise party.
8 And, of course, the cheerleader girlfriends of half the team.
9 I was pretty psyched about the whole thing really. And my
10 mom was going nuts.

11     She had things hidden in every closet of the house.
12 Every night she'd sneak and work on a video of pictures of
13 me growing up. The big day came and I graciously acted
14 totally clueless. My mother beamed. After cooking out,
15 cake, and all that jazz, she herded everyone into the living
16 room for the memory video presentation — on the *big* screen
17 TV. And that's when the fun stopped.

18     Mom had put a whole naked-baby-bathtub section in the
19 video and there were no appropriately placed black bars
20 covering anything. *Everyone* saw it! My buddies could not
21 stop pointing and laughing. To make things worse, Mom had
22 messed up the timing on a few of the slides and instead of
23 them briefly *flashing* — no pun intended — on the screen,
24 they hung up there for like a minute each! Do you know how
25 long a minute feels when your naked baby pictures are all
26 over a *big screen TV?* What in Pete's sake was my mother
27 thinking? How can I go to high school now?

# 21. Teenage Vampire

### (Guy)

1    "Where were you last night?"

2    It should've been an easy question, but when you're a
3 teenage vampire, nothing is easy. Your whole life is a series
4 of lies and cover-ups. Constantly weaving normal details
5 into an otherwise abnormal life.

6    But how can you tell the truth when history and vicious
7 rumors have given your kind a bad rap your entire
8 existence? Would anyone believe that you drank from a
9 blood bank instead of a human body? Or would they hide
10 their children and lock up their homes?

11    I'm not asking for pity. There are greater things in life to
12 feel sorrow over. Famine. Poverty. War. I would not expect
13 anyone to shed a tear over me. In many ways I have been
14 blessed, not cursed. Living with no sense of impending
15 death frees one to explore the many opportunities that life
16 has to offer. I've spent decades discovering art, music,
17 theatre. I've spent other decades exploring the wilder side:
18 Harleys, fast cars, and yes, fast women. I can reinvent
19 myself over and over again in any town in the world. I've
20 lived and seen more than anyone could possibly ever see in
21 a normal lifetime.

22    This being said, I have seen a great deal of people come
23 and go. Some did not leave this world quickly enough while
24 others seemed to take a piece of me with them. That is the
25 greatest tragedy of this condition: seeing far too many I
26 have loved grow old and die. By far it is the most
27 unbearable.

28    So in answer to the question, "Where was I last night?"

1   I was at home, alone, allowing my mind once again to dance
2   with the memories of a girl I once loved, wishing that when
3   she died I could've gone with her. But will I give that answer
4   to my latest friends? Of course not. My life is not, nor will
5   ever be, something a mere mortal can understand.

# 22. This Class Really Stinks!

(Girl)

1　When I say my English class really stinks, I mean it!
2　Mrs. Turntree has lost her mind. Did she honestly think she
3　could give the guys free rein over their bodily noises and
4　they wouldn't go completely crazy? It smells worse than a
5　public restroom in here. And that can of flowery scented
6　spray just makes things worse. It's so strong it makes your
7　eyes water. It's like trying to cover up a rotting body with a
8　squirt of perfume. You might as well call it "gross smell
9　spray" because that's what it's used for.

10　She might not have a sense of smell, but we sure do!
11　And what kind of bull is that, anyway? How can you *not* have
12　a sense of smell? She's got a nose, doesn't she? And it's no
13　small puppy either. With a honker like that she should be
14　smelling things from ten miles away!

15　*(Mimics.)* "As long as you don't disrupt class, it won't
16　bother me," she said. Well, by golly, it's bothering me. *A lot!*
17　And just because you can't hear them, doesn't mean you
18　can't smell them! These guys have mastered the art of
19　doing it quietly. If they spent half as much time focusing in
20　class as they do on that, they'd all be straight A students
21　instead of a bunch of smelly morons!

22　I think I'm going to switch to another class. They can't
23　make me stay in here under these conditions. Aren't there
24　laws about working conditions? Maybe I should file a
25　complaint. Or maybe I'll just sue the school. That's it! I'll
26　be the one student to make a stand! I'll be the voice of the
27　people! The voice for everyone in class who actually *has*
28　*class!* Mrs. Turntree is about to smell something and it's the
29　*smell of defeat!*

# 23. Anyone Got a Match?

## (Guy)

1      OK guys, listen up. I've got some great advice for you.
2  Never, ever, eat Mexican before going to your girlfriend's
3  house to watch a movie. And never, ever, after eating
4  Mexican should you eat a triple chocolate shake with extra
5  whipped cream, especially if you know that dairy products
6  do *not* always agree with you.

7      There I am. Arm around my girl. Snuggling on the
8  couch. When *wham!* The first pain hits. Total flinch. Pray
9  she didn't see. Another pain. A whopper of a pain! Cover by
10  bending over and acting like I'm going to sneeze. My
11  stomach is gurgling like crazy. I *know* she can hear it. Cover
12  by turning up the sound on the television and making up an
13  excuse about too much wax in my ears. OK, looking back,
14  that wasn't such a good cover, but think about it, which is
15  worse? A little earwax or admitting you're having some
16  serious gas pains? Right. So you understand.

17      Anyway, the pain keeps getting worse and worse until I
18  think — or rather I *know* — I am going to explode. Literally.
19  Only guess what, the *only* bathroom I'm allowed to use —
20  *(Mimics)* No boys allowed upstairs where the bedrooms are
21  — is the one attached to the family room. The room we're
22  in.

23      I go in. I cough a lot to hide the noise. I even sing a little
24  when necessary. I know without a doubt that she either
25  thinks I'm crazy, or she knows exactly what is going on.
26  Either way, not good for me.

27      But that's not the worst part. The absolute worst and
28  most embarrassing part is the smell. Like nothing you've

1 ever smelled before. Like dead, rotting corpses covered in
2 cow manure and baked in the sun. I am positive the smell
3 is not staying politely in the confines of the bathroom. In
4 fact, I am almost sure I can physically see it seeping out
5 underneath the door. I look around. There is nothing. No air
6 freshener. No perfume. No hair spray. No match to light.
7 Nothing. But seriously, it would take a match and maybe
8 some dynamite to cover up the smell. I hang out in there as
9 long as I can. First out of necessity, and then because
10 there's no way I can go out there!

11   I hear Amanda moving around. A cough. Then
12 whispering. She's talking to her parents. They don't know
13 what to do. Should they knock or not knock? I sit on the
14 floor and pray they don't knock. But they do.

15   I have no choice. I have to go out. I don't even look at
16 them. I say good-bye and run from the house. I break up
17 with Amanda the next day. And that is why I'm telling you,
18 my friends, never, ever eat Mexican before going over to your
19 girlfriend's house!

# 24. A Friend in Need

(Guy)

1  So there I was, handing out my "Vote for Scott" buttons
2  — he's my best friend and he's running for president of the
3  tenth grade class, so if you haven't voted yet, what are you
4  doing standing here listening to me? *Go!* Run! Get out of
5  here! What do you need, an *invitation?!* Go on!

6  *(Pause)* Oh ... dudes ... I forgot I was in the middle of my
7  whole story ... So anyway, there I was, looking all cool and
8  democratic and all and helping out my friend, 'cause that's
9  what friends do, when I saw her. The most beautiful girl in
10  the world. She's got this hair — yeah, well, of course she
11  has hair, right? But like her hair is different. And it was like
12  a flag waving in the wind. Yeah, that's right, a flag, man!

13  And then, she was walking right toward me, you know,
14  to get a button I guess. Only when I handed it to her my
15  hand was really hot and sweaty and so she dropped it right
16  there at my feet.

17  So I had to bend over to get it, only I shouldn't have
18  'cause my pants were squeezing a little too tight. Which
19  stinks 'cause they're my favorite pair of pants. I've had them
20  for five years or something crazy like that. But anyway, of
21  course they go *riiiip!* Like the loudest sound I've ever heard.
22  I tried to laugh it off. I mean, what choice did I have, right
23  dudes? But the look on that chick's face was pure disgust.
24  Not like your normal oh-that's-gross kind of disgusted look
25  but the I-am-seriously-going-to-puke-until-I-die kind of look.

26  That chick didn't even stick around long enough to take
27  the button.

28  Now I gotta tell my best friend that I not only lost the girl
29  of my dreams, I lost him a vote!

# 25. Bubble-Butt

(Girl)

1     I am the new advocate for a gum-free school! I'm
2  serious. Don't believe me? Look at my face. Do I look like
3  I'm kidding? After all these years of thinking the teachers
4  were just being controlling evil dictators who were being
5  completely power hungry, I am finally on their side! They're
6  right. Gum is evil. Gum should be banned. Gum should not
7  be allowed in schools. Kids can't handle the responsibility of
8  chewing gum. It's a distraction. The smacking. The
9  popping. All of it. They were right!
10    I'm going to write a letter to the principal. To the school
11  board. To the mayor. The governor. Maybe even to the
12  President of the United States. Gum should be banned from
13  everywhere, not just schools! Stores. The bowling alley.
14  Movie theatres. *The mall!* It should be like that Christmas
15  special where the mayor banned the toys. *No gum allowed*
16  *in the U.S. of A.!* Penalty by death! Or at the very least, a
17  few years in prison!
18    I bet I could get the dentists behind me. Other than it
19  might put them out of a job. Certainly the companies that
20  make mints would support me. Without gum chewing
21  allowed, mint sales would skyrocket! They might even name
22  a new mint flavor after me. I could be their new
23  spokesperson!
24    In fact, I'll become so famous for being the anti-gum girl
25  that no one in their right mind would dare to call me *bubble-*
26  *butt* ever again! That's right. You heard me. You stupid,
27  moronic, childish people out there that think it's *so funny*
28  that some disrespectful punk of a kid was too lazy to

1   actually get up and *throw* his gum in the trash, so lazy that
2   he thought it was OK to put a chewed up wad of gum and
3   *spit* on the seat — the same seat I just happened to sit on
4   — oh yeah, you people think it's so funny to now call me
5   bubble-butt! Well, I'll be so famous I won't even remember
6   who you are! So put *that* in your mouth and *pop it!*

# 26. Where's the White Bread?

(Guy)

1     Our house has gone brown. Not green like the majority
2  of the world. You know, reuse and recycle. Save the earth.
3  Bring your own bag to the grocery. That kind of thing. *That*
4  I could handle. But no, we're not green in our house. We're
5  brown. Ugly, nasty, gross-tasting brown. Everything we eat
6  is either whole wheat, whole grain, or some sort of fancy
7  fiber. I was fine when it was just the bread. Put enough
8  peanut butter and jelly on it and you can disguise anything.
9  But then the brown invaded every aspect of our cupboards
10 and our fridge. Like an army of aliens, the brown has taken
11 over my house.
12     The spaghetti noodles were the last straw. Noodles
13 should *not* be brown! They taste like soggy slivers of a
14 cardboard box. I would drown them out with sauce, but it's
15 no better! Low-fat, low-sodium, low-sugar, low-carb, low-
16 calorie, all natural ingredients! I don't *want all natural*
17 *ingredients!* I want the fake, great tasting, chemically built
18 stuff that looks, smells, and *tastes* like spaghetti!
19     Do you have any idea how tasteless food can be when
20 they've taken all the good stuff out of it? Well, come to my
21 house. You'll find out real quick. I mean, seriously, what
22 good are chips if they don't have fat in them? Or ice cream
23 without *sugar?!* You might as well eat a chunk of solid milk.
24 But even that isn't sacred in our house. Oh no. We've got
25 *soy* everything. I can't even begin to tell you how nasty
26 cereal is when you pour soy milk over it. Of course the
27 cereal is so full of fiber it swells up like a sponge. I promise
28 you, my cereal is so thick I could eat it with a fork.

1      Look at me! I'm practically skin and bones. Not because
2    I'm losing fat from eating healthy. I'm skinny because I'm
3    *starving!* It's time for a revolution! *Down with brown! Down*
4    *with brown! Down with brown!*

# 27. Never Wear Your Sister's Pants

(Guy)

1   First of all, I would like to clarify that my sister is an
2   athlete. She has tons of sweatpants. Normal, athletic
3   sweatpants. Unisex pants for guys *or* girls. That's what unisex
4   means, right? Well, that's why I didn't think anything about
5   grabbing a pair of her sweats out of her drawer when I found
6   I had *no* clean sweats and *no* clean jeans to my name.

7   By the way, thanks Mom: "I will *not* pick clothes off your
8   floor and put them in the washer. If you want them clean,
9   you can at least put them in the laundry basket and walk
10  them down the hall to the laundry room."

11  Anyway, so I grabbed the black pants out of my sister's
12  drawer. No big deal. Figured *no one* would ever know. Hey,
13  not even *her* if I put them back before she noticed. Don't
14  look all disgusted, you know you've done the same thing
15  before! But I was *wrong* about the whole no-one-would-ever-
16  know thing. I made it through *three* classes before I found
17  out I had the word *flirt* in big pink letters across my
18  backside!

19  And just so you know, feel free to spread the word that
20  I no longer have *any* friends in first, second, or third period!
21  I mean seriously, people, you weren't even going to tell me?
22  In fact, not only did my supposed "friends" *not* tell me, they
23  secretly took video on their phones and sent it to everyone
24  in school! How do you think I found out? Someone was
25  stupid enough to actually send it to *me* by mistake! I'm sure
26  it will be on YouTube before the day is over.

27  Well, take a little piece of advice from the new flirt of
28  Jackson County High School, never *ever* borrow your sister's
29  pants!

# 28. Living in a Bubble

(Girl)

1  My parents are in need of some serious therapy. Or
2  medication. Or both. I'm not being funny either. Don't
3  believe me? Look at this. Do you have any idea what *this* is?
4  Of course you don't. No one in their right mind would know
5  what this is! That's because your normal, average,
6  completely sane-minded parents would never dream of
7  buying ... wait for it ... *a mattress sensor!*
8      That's right. You heard me. My crazy, obsessed,
9  controlling, psychotic parents have bought me a mattress
10 sensor. Know what it's for? Of course you don't! Well, I'll tell
11 you. It's a handy little gadget that overprotective parents of
12 *itty bitty babies* buy so that if the baby doesn't move every
13 twenty seconds, it goes off! Like a fire alarm. My lovely
14 parents have bought one so that when they tuck me in at
15 night — yes, you heard me right — they can activate the
16 alarm and then if someone snatches me — oh yes, you
17 heard that right, too! — they can come and rescue me.
18     The worst part is, they've been this way my whole life!
19 When I was a baby, baby knee pads. Seriously. They didn't
20 want my knees getting scuffed while I learned to crawl. It got
21 better. Baby helmet when I started walking. My baby
22 pictures look like I've had brain surgery. My little neck can
23 barely hold up my head!
24     My parents were way past the safety plug things people
25 stick in their sockets. Way past the door latches and toilet
26 latches and prescription safety bottle caps. Way past any
27 sense of reason. Every vaccination ever made I've had.
28 Never mind that it's only for people in the far reaches of the

1    world. I've had it!
2        I might as well forget about driving. They can't possibly
3    make a car with enough air bags to suit my parents. I swear,
4    I might as well live in a bubble!

# 29. Motto Mom

(Girl)

1    My mother is driving me crazy. One minute she's Active
2  Mom. The next she's Motto Mom. It's like she's reading
3  health books and parenting books before bed every night
4  and figuring out exactly how to be the most annoying
5  mother she can be. All these years of being more or less
6  normal and now it's after dinner walks, hikes on Sundays,
7  which I specifically think are reserved for napping, and
8  badminton before the sun goes down. It's like she can't sit
9  still.

10  Where's the mom I knew and loved that liked to come
11  home from work and crash on the couch? Sleep in on
12  Saturdays? Didn't own a sports bra and never, ever would've
13  dared to suggest that an early morning workout would be
14  "refreshing." Refreshing?! What part of sweating your butt
15  off on the treadmill for an hour is refreshing? I thought the
16  six cups of coffee she had in the morning was refreshing!
17  But, oh no. She kicked that habit!

18  Worst part is, when Active Mom wears out, she morphs
19  into Motto Mom. You can't stop the advice from pouring out
20  of her. Cliché after cliché on life in general, politics, the
21  earth — you name it, Mom's got a saying for it. She wants
22  to talk about every little detail of my life, analyze it, and then
23  tell me what to do about it. Where was she in middle school
24  when I actually *wanted* to talk to her? Now? Forget it. I'm
25  not sharing my innermost thoughts with her, especially not
26  while she's got me running on a treadmill!

27  Well, just like Superman has kryptonite, there has to be
28  something that turns Active Mom and Motto Mom back into

1    Normal Mom. Wait a minute! I've got it. *(Pause)* Hey, Mom!
2    Look what I've got ... a big cup of freshly made coffee ...
3    mmmm ... oh does it smell good?

# 30. Me and Mr. Benchwarmer?

(Girl)

1     I think I'm going to break up with my boyfriend. Not that
2  he's done anything wrong. I mean it's not really his fault, but
3  I feel like I've been scammed. You know how sometimes
4  there's this thing you really, really want and then you get it
5  and it's not what you expected? Or it's broken or
6  something? Well that's exactly what happened to me. When
7  I said yes to Philip he was the star quarterback of the
8  football team. The star!

9     In the three weeks I've been his girlfriend he broke his
10 finger, his toe, *and* chipped a tooth! I'm serious! Who has
11 that kind of luck? I mean seriously, what are the odds of
12 that happening to someone? He's gone from star
13 quarterback to benchwarmer. Now don't look at me like
14 that. I *know* it's not his fault and I *know* it shouldn't matter,
15 but let's get real here, it does! Face it, I might as well be
16 dating a member of the band now.

17     The way I see it, I've got perfect grounds to break up
18 with him. My dad's a lawyer and he talks about breach of
19 contract all the time. Well, that's what this is! Philip can't
20 just change the terms of our contract. Think about it. What
21 if you had a boyfriend with really great hair. You know,
22 underwear model hair and abs! And all of a sudden he
23 shaved his head and his abs turned to flab? You'd drop him
24 in a heartbeat! Well, this is no different.

25     Oh great, here comes Mr. Benchwarmer hobbling down
26 the hall now. Guess I'd better go break the news to him
27 before he breaks something else!

# 31. Do As I Say, Not As I Do
(Guy)

1      So my boss is the biggest hypocrite I've ever known.
2 She strolls in here every day over a half hour late — no
3 apology, no explanation, nothing! Just waltzes in like she
4 owns the place. And then when I come in late three measly
5 little times, she writes me up! Puts me on warning! Wanna
6 know how many minutes late I was the last time? Two
7 minutes! Two stinking little minutes! My watch said I was on
8 time. The clock to punch in on says I was late. Well, who's
9 to say that the punch-in clock is right? Maybe it runs fast!
10 Maybe they make it run fast on purpose just so they can
11 write people up. But even if I was two minutes late, how can
12 she look at me with a straight face and talk about my
13 tardiness issue when she hasn't been on time one day in
14 months?!
15      Oh, and then to add icing to the cake, she wrote me up
16 for not cleaning the popcorn machine well enough. That's
17 crazy! I scrubbed that thing until the copper bottom shined!
18 And I even cut my finger digging a kernel out of the bottom.
19 But do I get any thanks for that? Of course not. Not only did
20 she tell me I didn't clean it well enough, she said I took too
21 long to do it. Too long! How would she know? Her precious
22 manicured fingers have *never* cleaned a popcorn machine in
23 her life. Nor a counter. Nor a window. Nor a floor. And
24 definitely *not* a bathroom. Heaven forbid she should ever
25 scrub a toilet!
26      I have a theory, though. I think she and the owner are
27 dating. I've caught them being all flirty and everything. Well,
28 that would explain a lot, wouldn't it? No wonder Miss Thing

1    can waltz around here like a princess criticizing everyone
2    and never lifting a finger! I tell you what, I'm going to do
3    everything I can to expose her true colors.

# 32. Concert Curfew
(Guy)

1    Why do I even bother to work hard to make money that
2  my girlfriend just flushes down the toilet? OK, to be fair,
3  she isn't exactly the one pushing down the handle — it's
4  that crazy father of hers! Does he have any idea how many
5  months I had to save in order to buy those concert tickets
6  in the first place? A concert I've been waiting to go to for
7  three years!

8    For three years, I've been waiting. So what happens? I
9  actually get the tickets! Great seats, too. I didn't even care
10 that they were almost one hundred dollars apiece. I knew I
11 wanted to go and of course I wanted Ashley to go with me.
12 It's her favorite band, too.

13    Of course, if I'd known her father was going to be
14 completely unreasonable, I might have rethought my guest
15 selection. Or if I'd known that they'd have the biggest car
16 pileup on I-22 that caused the concert being delayed by over
17 an hour. Or if I'd known that Ashley's father would *not*
18 budge on her normal curfew.

19    She wouldn't even call and ask him! Said she knew what
20 he would say. Well, wasn't it worth a shot? I bet if it were
21 her money being thrown out the window, she would've called
22 him. Truth is, I think she wanted to go home. All because I
23 wouldn't buy her a T-shirt. It's not that I didn't want to. But
24 come on. Two hundred bucks on tickets made me broke!

25    I tell you what, next time my favorite band comes to
26 town, I'm only getting one ticket!

# 33. Bad Grades = No License
(Guy)

1     This is the worst day of my life. I studied like crazy to
2    pass the written part of my driving test and it paid off! I
3    actually passed. Well, not to brag, but I not only passed, I
4    aced it! One hundred percent. Probably the only test I've
5    ever aced in my life, and so what do I find out right after
6    that? It doesn't matter! They won't let me get my license.
7    How can that be? I didn't even miss one question.

8    So they hand me this paper that tells me this stupid new
9    law about bad grades equals no license. Is that even legal?
10  Don't I have rights? Doesn't every sixteen-year-old have the
11  right to drive? What do grades have to do with the ability to
12  drive? Just because I don't study or do homework doesn't
13  mean I won't know to stop at a stop sign or obey the speed
14  limit. I might be lazy, but I'm not a moron!

15  And obviously I can study. I made a one hundred
16  percent. Doesn't that count for something? I think this is a
17  joke. A way to oppress the American teenager! Other
18  countries don't do this, do they? As a matter of fact, I think
19  some countries, even some states, let kids drive at fifteen.
20  *Fifteen!* They'll let some little fifteen-year-old drive and not
21  me! Just because I got a couple of Ds on my report card?
22  What if I was just stupid? They can't penalize someone for
23  being stupid, can they?

24  I want a lawyer, that's what I want. An advocate for all
25  the students out there like me! Students who have a right
26  to drive! Students who can learn but choose not to!
27  Students who might not like homework, but can operate a
28  car with their eyes closed!

1    OK, wait. I didn't mean that part. Of course I would
2  never drive with my eyes closed. Oh, come on! *Please* just
3  give me my license!

# 34. Is That Spinach?

(Girl)

1    You won't believe this, but ever since I got my first
2    boyfriend, I have had this recurring dream at least once a
3    week. It haunts me even when I'm not sleeping. I relive it
4    over and over every day in my head. I know it's ridiculous. I
5    probably need therapy or something, right? What kind of
6    normal person has the same dream over and over?
7        The dream is exactly the same every time. There I am,
8    in this beautiful red cocktail dress. My hair is up. My
9    makeup looks great. Obviously I'm going on a really special
10   date. Not just a jeans-and-shirt movie night, but a real
11   fancy gotta-tip-the-waiter date. Everything starts out great.
12   The guy shows up at my door, flowers in hand, just like in
13   the movies. We head out in his ultra-cool convertible sports
14   car. My hair flows in the wind and still looks great when we
15   arrive at the restaurant. It's like the best night of my life.
16       And then it happens. Out of nowhere. Middle of dinner
17   he's gazing into my eyes and all of a sudden his face
18   contorts in horror. Like he's seen something he'll never
19   recover from. I watch in total confusion as he frantically
20   motions for the waiter. He pays quickly and rushes me out
21   the door. I don't know what else to do but sit in silence as
22   he careens his fancy car through the streets back to my
23   house.
24       He screeches to a halt in my driveway. Mumbles
25   something to the effect, "I'll call you." But I know it's a lie.
26   Even in my dream I know he's never going to call me.
27   Something is terribly wrong. I rush inside as he squeals his
28   tires backing out of the driveway. He can't get away from me

1    fast enough.

2    In the bathroom I study my face. What could possibly
3    have caused the look of pure disgust? Nothing. I smile. And
4    there it is. A piece of spinach the size of a small country
5    stuck in between my two front teeth.

6    I know it's stupid! I know it's crazy. I don't even eat
7    spinach for crying out loud! But that dream has scarred me
8    for life! I swear I will never eat in front of a guy for my whole
9    entire life!

# 35. Sloppy Work
(Girl)

1     My teacher is going to give me an F on this report. I just
2 know it. She's going to take one look at these blurry letters
3 and ink smudges and think I turned in a sloppy paper on
4 purpose. But it's not my fault! It's hers. I swear.

5     How can she be allowed to force me to write a
6 mandatory paper on such a horrible topic? I don't want to
7 read about animal abuse. Don't I have rights? Why would
8 anyone with half a heart want to read about horrible things
9 and then write about them? What kind of coldhearted
10 person does she think I am? I can't stop crying!

11     Who could do such horrible things to such loveable
12 animals? They're helpless and trusting. Just look at the
13 pictures of their little cuddly faces. What kind of sick person
14 takes advantage of that? And what kind of sick teacher
15 forces her students to read about such horrors? Such
16 atrocities? That's what I'd like to know.

17     This one woman was hoarding cats. She said she was
18 just trying to take care of them so they wouldn't be out in
19 the wild, but she had over one-hundred cats in her house.
20 They were everywhere. I can't even imagine how bad her
21 house smelled. And that's one of the nicer stories! Believe
22 me, there are some really sick people out there.

23     I've had nightmares for a week. And now — look at this
24 ... this wreck of a paper! Even after all the suffering I've gone
25 through to write this, I know she's going to fail me. She
26 should not be allowed to make a report like this mandatory!

27     The world is so unfair. She should be the one getting an
28 F. An F for *fired!*

# 36. Boyfriend's Creepy Mother
## (Girl)

1     OK, I'm just going to say it. And you might want to
2  break up with me once I do, but I just can't keep this
3  bottled up inside me anymore. I've tried. Believe me, I've
4  tried to look past it all, to remind myself that I love you and
5  not your family. That nothing else is important. But ... I've
6  just got to be honest here and come right out with it: Your
7  mom is crazy. And not the fun kind of crazy that lets you
8  drive when you're fifteen, or takes you to all night bowling
9  on a school night, or even sneaks you into R-rated movies.
10  But crazy-crazy.

11     Do you know what she did the other day? She called me.
12  OK, not so bad, right? If she just needed to ask me a quick
13  question or something. But she called me to *chat*. Like we're
14  friends. But that's not even the crazy part. She wanted to
15  know what size underwear I wear. She wanted to buy me
16  some.

17     *(Pause)* No! That's not sweet. It's *creepy!* I'm not her
18  daughter. I don't want my boyfriend's *mother* buying me
19  underwear. Seriously, don't you see anything wrong with
20  that?

21     And get this. Then she wanted to know what my favorite
22  color was. Want to know why? So she could buy us — not
23  you and I "us" but *her and I* "us" — matching shirts to wear
24  to your family reunion this weekend.

25     So let's get two things straight. Number one, I do not
26  want to chat with your mother about my underwear, and
27  two, I do *not* wear matching *anything* with *anyone*,
28  especially not your *mother!*

# 37. Get Out and Stay Out!

(Girl)

1   I thought going to college meant that my sister was
2   going to be out of my hair. That finally it would be my turn
3   to have Mom and Dad to myself. Isn't she supposed to be
4   off having the time of her life and not thinking twice about
5   us? Isn't she supposed to be spreading her wings, cutting
6   the cord, or untying the apron strings?

7   Why is it then that every Friday afternoon by the time I
8   get home from school, my sister's car is parked by the curb
9   in front of our house? It's been four months and she hasn't
10  missed a weekend yet! Why does she even bother to leave?
11  She's like a boomerang that just keeps coming right back!

12  I'll walk in and she'll say, "Did you miss me?" Miss her?
13  By the time I realize she's actually gone, she's back! How
14  could I possibly miss her?

15  Well, not me! When I leave for college, I am leaving.
16  Going. Going. Gone. Adios. Don't look back. No regrets and
17  all that! You won't see my face every weekend. Heck no! I
18  *might* come home for the holidays — those just wouldn't be
19  the same alone! And maybe a couple of weekends when Dad
20  does the fire pit because I love those cheese dogs cooked on
21  a stick over the fire and the toasted marshmallows. I
22  definitely would not want to miss that! And maybe when it's
23  someone's birthday, or maybe even when Mom does one of
24  her all weekend scrapbooking events, because I'll have lots
25  to scrapbook once I'm in college.

26  But other than that, I am staying at school!

# 38. Better Than the Movies
(Guy)

1   Going to school is better than going to the movies. I
2   mean it. You don't see this much action in an Arnold
3   Schwarzenegger movie. There's kicking, shoving, slapping,
4   punching, knock-downs. You name it. Sometimes there's
5   even blood or broken bones! One time a guy lost two teeth!
6   It's crazy! You can't go down the hall, walk to the bus, or go
7   to lunch without getting a prime view of some sort of action.
8       The cat fights between the girls are the best. Hair
9   pulling, name-calling, scratching. You should see the
10  fingernails on some of these chicks. They're like weapons!
11  They shouldn't be allowed to walk around with those things.
12  And sometimes if we're really lucky, there's some clothes
13  ripping to go along with it. One girl ended up in her bra when
14  it was all said and done. You'd think her losing her shirt
15  would be enough to make her stop fighting, but thankfully
16  no! She kept right on swinging. You go, girl.
17      You can't make this stuff up. These girls are potential
18  Jerry Springer guests! I could easily see chairs flying
19  through the air. I don't know why the teachers feel the need
20  to break it up. I say let them fight to the death. OK, not
21  really to the death, but at least until I have to leave and go
22  back to class.

# 39. On a Break

(Girl)

1     It all makes perfect sense now. It wasn't me at all. I
2  didn't suddenly grow warts or put off some guy repellent.
3  There's a perfectly good explanation why I've been dateless
4  for over three months. Why no one asked me to
5  homecoming. Or to the movies. Or out to eat. Or anywhere!
6  Why I've been sitting home alone every Friday and Saturday
7  night.

8     It was my stupid ex-boyfriend. He's been telling everyone
9  we're on a break. A break! Meaning, of course, that I'm off-
10 limits because we're supposedly getting back together as
11 soon as we work things out.

12    Here's a newsflash: It's not true, people! Shane and I are
13 not on a break. We're *over*. O-v-e-r! As in *never* getting back
14 together. He cheated on me ... with my best friend! Does he
15 really think I'll ever forget that? Or forgive him for that? No
16 way! And a break definitely isn't going to make me want to
17 be with him. Not unless by break he means I get to break
18 every bone in his body!

19    Where did he even get that idea? I was perfectly clear
20 when I broke up with him. In no way did I insinuate that I
21 just needed some "time alone" or "breathing space" or
22 whatever bull he told everyone. I can breathe just fine.
23 Better, in fact, now that I'm not with him.

24    So let's set the record straight. Everyone spread the
25 word: Shane and I are *not* on a break. We're broken! As in
26 can *never* be fixed!

27    Now would somebody *please* ask me out?!

# 40. Note Taking or Not?

## (Guy)

1    My teacher has lost her mind. Or rather she can't make
2 up her mind. One minute she's telling us to take good notes
3 and write everything she says down in our notebooks. Then
4 when she sees us frantically trying to write everything she's
5 saying, she says, "You don't need to write that down." So
6 we stop and a few moments later when she sees that we're
7 *not* taking notes, she yells at us for being lazy and asks why
8 we're not writing things down.

9    Here's the real kicker: The stuff she tells us not to write
10 down is what keeps showing up on the tests! It's like she's
11 trying to trick us or play mind games with us.

12    Maybe she's bipolar. Or the female version of Dr. Jekyll
13 and Mr. Hyde. She seems so clueless when we say, "But
14 you told us not to write that down." She gets all sarcastic
15 and says, "Yeah, like I would tell you not to write that down.
16 Do you have any idea how important that is? Of course you
17 need to write that down!"

18    It's so unfair. It's like taking a class from a
19 schizophrenic! She's totally got a split personality. Surely
20 they can't hold us responsible for not learning from a crazy
21 like her. But apparently they do because the principal says
22 she's an excellent teacher. Of course he's never sat in on
23 any of her classes to see how nuts she is!

24    Well, if nothing else, I've learned this: I don't care how
25 many times she tells me *not* to write something down, I'm
26 doing it anyway. In fact, I'm doing the exact opposite of
27 whatever she tells me so that maybe I'll get the right
28 information and pass her stupid test!

# 41. Backpack Burdens
(Guy)

1  Look at this book. Look how thick it is! It's over three
2  inches thick, maybe even four! It's got over four hundred
3  pages and it weighs about five pounds. So what's the big
4  deal, right? I've got a big, fat book — so what? Well, guess
5  what? I've got four more like this baby in my backpack.
6  That's twenty pounds or more that I'm packing around every
7  day on my back. Like a farm mule or something.

8  Look at me! I only weigh a hundred pounds. I'm carrying
9  twenty percent of my weight around every day. No wonder
10 my back is killing me. I've had to start going to a
11 chiropractor and everything and I'm only fourteen-years-old.
12 I'll probably have to have back surgery before I'm twenty!

13 When I finally get to take my backpack off, after a long
14 walk from the bus stop to my house, I'm all bent over like
15 the hunchback of Notre Dame. Or a hundred-year-old man!
16 I can't imagine another three years of this. And then there's
17 college! How am I going to survive that?

18 It's so pointless, too. I mean, come on. Are we really
19 going to cover four hundred pages of *anything* in one
20 semester? Even in one year? Doubt it. We probably won't go
21 over even half this stuff. But just try not bringing your book
22 to class and you get a detention. Doesn't even matter if we
23 crack the thing open or not. It's like they're in cahoots with
24 the doctors and chiropractors.

25 Enough is enough! Today I'm going shopping for one of
26 those backpacks with wheels!

# 42. No Caffeine?

(Guy)

1      This time they have crossed a line! It was bad enough
2 when they instituted no jeans in the dress code two years
3 ago. And then last year's flip-flop rule — meaning no flip-
4 flops allowed — just about pushed me over the edge. But
5 now? Have they completely lost their minds or do they just
6 sit around trying to think of ways to torment us?
7      No caffeine in the soda machines? How do they expect
8 us to stay awake? They give us tons of homework that
9 makes us stay up half the night and now they want to take
10 away our caffeine? Oh, they can say it's all about
11 incorporating wellness into the school, but it's a lie! I don't
12 see the teachers giving up their precious caffeine! My history
13 teacher drinks at least four cups of Joe in my class alone. I
14 say if we have to give it up, they do too. Talk about a bunch
15 of hypocrites!
16      Truth is, they just don't want us hyped up on caffeine.
17 It's their underhanded way of keeping us sedated. Like little
18 learning robots they can control. Next thing you know they'll
19 be taking away all the sugar. No candy bars or sports
20 drinks. And when that doesn't work, they'll take all the
21 carbs — no chips or crackers!
22      Well, with no sugar, carbs, or caffeine, I'll be sleeping
23 through every class. So let me just tell you, if you expect
24 me to stay awake, you'd better make this a *whole* lot more
25 interesting!

# 43. Cougar Mom

(Girl)

1     My mom is becoming a Cougar. Right before my very
2  eyes. I've seen her transform from the woman in the "mom
3  jeans" to the Cougar in the tightest pants you've ever seen!
4     I'm so embarrassed. I can't even bring my friends home
5  any more. I've seen the way she looks at the guys. It's sick!
6  Doesn't she have any idea how ridiculous this all is? She's
7  in her forties! Not twenties!
8     She says she's just trying to be a cool mom. The kind
9  that doesn't embarrass her daughter by wearing curlers in
10  her hair, having a pot belly, and wearing a ratty old
11  bathrobe. Well, mission *not* accomplished! You might not be
12  in curlers, but I'm mortified that my mom looks like she'd
13  be comfortable around a stripper pole.
14     That is *so* not cool, Mom. You're twenty-four years older
15  than me, and contrary to what you think, I do not like it
16  when people say that we look like sisters! Oh, I *know* you
17  do. You don't stop smiling for hours when that happens.
18     But how do you think I feel? Think about it. Do you want
19  to look like *your* mother? I didn't think so. And just
20  because you've been working out and working hard to tune
21  that body up doesn't mean everyone needs to see it! A little
22  modesty, please. You might have the body of a teenager, but
23  you're *not* a teenager. Your belly-showing days are over!
24  O-v-e-r!
25     Got it? So get rid of your tight pants and let's go
26  shopping to get you some respectable middle-aged woman's
27  clothes!

# 44. We High-Five
## (Girl)

1  Some people should never be allowed on the other side
2  of a camera. Especially when it's a video camera. Have you
3  seen the latest school announcement? *We High-Five?* It is
4  the lamest thing I've ever seen. Not only is the acting bad,
5  you can't possibly sit through it without laughing
6  hysterically — the content is hilarious!

7  First, they zoom in on this couple in some serious lip-
8  lock. Then a big red X flashes across them on the screen.
9  Next, they show a couple going in for the kiss and right
10 before their lips meet, they back off and say, "Here at our
11 school we respect our teachers and fellow students, so we
12 high-five!" Then they smile real big and high-five each other.
13 The last slide says, "No PDA."

14 It's the most juvenile thing I've ever seen. Do they really
15 think for a minute that this student-made pathetic
16 infomercial is going to stop PDA in our school? It makes me
17 want to get a boyfriend just so I can make out! Heck, I may
18 not even wait until I have a boyfriend, it makes me so mad!

19 I don't know how they could even convince students to
20 be in it. Were the poor kids serving out a detention sentence
21 or something? I mean, maybe I could see being in the first
22 part when they're making out, but seriously, "we high-five?"
23 What are we? Kindergarteners?

# 45. Mom Never Cooks
## (Guy)

1     Most kids would kill to live at my house. We've got more
2 junk food in our cabinets and in our fridge than a boy's
3 dorm at college! Every kind of chip, cookie, cracker, ice
4 cream, frozen dinner, frozen pizza, and bag of candy —
5 we've got it. And I used to love it, too. Back when those
6 things were just snacks. But now that my mom has gotten
7 on the lazy train, those things are dinner! All we ever eat is
8 junk food, fast food, or grab-it — meaning anything you can
9 grab and fix yourself because Mom's not cooking!

10     Everyone I know would love to eat out six days a week.
11 Not me. I'm sick of it. A guy can only eat so many burgers
12 and fries and buckets of chicken. Everything we eat is fried.
13 I can't remember the last time I ate a vegetable. A real one.
14 And no, French fries don't count.

15     So what'd I go and do? I made the major mistake of
16 telling my mom that I was sick of eating out. Now it's been
17 four weeks of home-cooked meals and no junk food. Not one
18 bag of chips left in the house. Not one morsel of candy.
19 Nothing. My snippy little comment about junk food spurred
20 some kind of health food frenzy! Now everything is fat-free
21 or calorie-reduced.

22     I never thought I'd say this, but I miss grab-it!

# 46. What If They See Me?

## (Girl)

1    So there's this new girl. She's not exactly what you'd
2  call pretty. In fact, not to be mean, but she's what my
3  grandma calls *homely*. Which she immediately follows up
4  with, "Bless her heart." Like that makes it OK to call
5  someone ugly. But anyway, I see this girl sitting alone every
6  day at lunch. There's always at least three empty chairs on
7  either side of her like people think she's contagious or
8  something. People stare and whisper to each other. They
9  don't even try to hide it or keep their voices low.

10    She keeps her head down and stares at her food. I know
11  she can hear what they're saying. Heck, everyone in the
12  lunch room can. And I feel so bad for her. Probably because
13  I remember being her. Long before contacts and braces and
14  a good hair stylist, I *was* that girl. But here's the thing. I
15  worked hard to get where I am. I did my time. Did my
16  suffering. I know the right thing to do is to reach out to the
17  poor girl. To sit beside her and start a conversation like I
18  wished so many times someone would have done with me.
19  I *know* all this and yet something holds me back.

20    What if someone *sees* me? What if everything I've worked
21  so hard for was ruined? What if they started talking about
22  me? How could I go through that all over again?

23    *(Pause)* But look at her. How can I just let her sit there
24  alone like that?

25    *(Pause. Take a few steps.)* Hi, my name's Melissa. What's
26  yours?

73

# 47. First Day Jitters
(Girl)

1   I know it's not cool to admit this, but I am *so* excited
2   about school starting tomorrow! It's my first day of high
3   school, how could I not be excited? And I know my friends
4   are, too. They just won't admit it. Everyone is trying to act
5   like they don't care in the least that we are starting one of
6   the most important chapters of our lives.
7   We all bought new clothes over the past few weeks, but
8   no one will dare wear them tomorrow. You have to wait a few
9   weeks for stuff like that. And don't even dream of wearing
10  new sneakers or everyone will know about it. You can't even
11  seem excited. That's completely uncool. You have to act
12  nonchalant — wear old clothes like it's no big deal. Well, it
13  *is* a big deal! We're in *high school now!* Why can't we act
14  excited about that?
15  I got new school supplies, too, but can't bring them. Not
16  right away. I have to smuggle them in with some old stuff
17  so I don't look like I'm trying too hard. I don't want people
18  thinking I'm some sort of school geek. I miss the days of
19  new school clothes, fresh new crayons, a new haircut, and
20  pictures with my backpack.
21  Wonder if I could wear my jean skirt? It's not all that
22  new and it looks kind of worn ... *no!* I can't wear a *skirt* on
23  the first day. That would be *so* pathetic. And how can I do
24  my hair without it looking like I'm trying too hard? I could
25  wear my new jeans. They're the kind with the rips so you
26  can't really tell that they're new ... not really. Oh, this is so
27  complicated!
28  How am I going to look like I don't care when I really,
29  really do?!

# 48. Too Old for Trick or Treat
(Girl)

1    My boyfriend seriously needs to grow up! He's like the
2    epitome of Peter Pan. He thinks he never needs to grow up.
3    Do you know what he did last night? He went trick-or-
4    treating. Like a little kid! I can't imagine what the people
5    thought when they opened their door and saw him standing
6    there, bag in hand! They probably wanted to slam their door
7    in fear. He is six feet tall, after all. It's not like he blends in.
8    I'm sure they were afraid he was going to rob them or
9    something. They probably watched him from behind their
10   blinds just to make sure he wasn't up to something. But the
11   sad thing is, he wasn't! I can totally understand going out
12   at his age to pull a couple of pranks. You know, TP a house
13   or two. Smash a few pumpkins. Maybe even steal a little
14   candy. But to actually go out trick-or-treating? Come on!
15   You should've seen his face later when he dumped out
16   his bag of goodies. He even separated his candy into little
17   piles. Gum in one. Chocolate in another. He even made a
18   pile of stuff he didn't like. Just like my little sister does. And
19   then he guarded the good piles to make sure I didn't take
20   anything.
21   He wasn't even embarrassed! Told me I was crazy for not
22   going, too. "It's free candy!" he told me. "Why wouldn't you
23   go?"
24   Why? Why?! Because I have an ounce of self-respect,
25   that's why! Next year if we're still dating, I'll *buy* him some
26   candy! And if he wants to dress up, we'll go to a party. It's
27   time for that boy to grow up!

# 49. No Ice Cream

(Girl)

1    My doctor has lost his mind! No dairy for a month?! How
2  is that even possible? Dairy is my life! Did you know that ice
3  cream is considered dairy? *Ice cream?!* I can't live without ice
4  cream for thirty days. Did you know there are seven hundred
5  and twenty hours in thirty days? Nobody on earth can go
6  that many hours without ice cream!

7    And cheese. Cheese is dairy. Even the fake looking stuff.
8  Even the stuff in a can! How can I eat a salad, or a hot hog,
9  or a grilled cheese sandwich without cheese?! It's
10 impossible!

11    I say the guy's a quack. Completely off his rocker. No
12 doctor should ever tell someone to live without dairy. What
13 about that slogan about milk doing a body good? How am I
14 going to eat my cookies? With water? Or soda? Is the man
15 really trying to get me to drink more *soda?*

16    My mother thinks he's a genius. But I say she's just
17 using this to punish me. It's like her evil way of getting back
18 at me for every bad thing I've ever done. A month without
19 dairy is the worst form of torture. Take my TV. Take my
20 video games. You can even take my cell phone, but not my
21 ice cream!

22    They say it's for my own good. That they're only trying
23 to help me. But I'd rather have my stomach hurt than this!
24 Isn't there a pill or something I can take? How am I
25 supposed to get the calcium I need? I'm a growing girl. This
26 could stunt my growth! My bones will be brittle. Just wait.
27 You'll see. I'll be breaking bones all over the place!

# 50. Too Much Too Soon
## (Girl)

1    I never thought I'd say this, but my boyfriend is *too*
2 sweet. In fact, if he was any sweeter, I think I would vomit
3 from sugar overload. He's like three pillowcases full of
4 Halloween candy. Or triple, triple chocolate cake. Or a
5 caramel apple with sprinkles. Or, OK, you get the point,
6 right? I always thought the sweeter the better. What's not to
7 love, right? Compliments all the time. Love notes. Small
8 gifts left in my locker. Who wouldn't love all that? Honestly.
9 He says I love you more than Mr. Harrison says "stop
10 talking." And believe me, that's a lot.

11    You think it'd be incredibly awesome being so adored,
12 but it's not! It's making me crazy. I feel like I've got a puppy
13 yapping around my feet just waiting for me to throw it a
14 bone of affection. It's not sweet at all. It's pathetic! Girls
15 don't want doormats. They want a guy who acts like a guy.
16 A little rough around the edges.

17    All this niceness makes me want to take advantage of
18 him just because I can. He's made it clear that he'd do
19 anything for me. So why shouldn't he do all my homework?
20 Or come over and do all my chores? OK, I'm not *that* mean.
21 Really, I'm not.

22    But last night he crossed a line. The guy wrote a song
23 about me! A. Song. About. Me. It should be so sweet, right?
24 But it's *lame!* I mean, really, we've only been dating *two*
25 *days!* Dude, get a grip!

# 51. Football Widow

(Girl)

1 The man of my dreams is finally mine! Mine after two
2 years of wishing and doing everything I could to get him to
3 notice me. And it's everything I dreamed it would be. The
4 stares as we walk down the hallway together. The whispers
5 when he kisses me at the door to my class. All my friends
6 are *so* jealous! And why wouldn't they be? I've got the most
7 popular guy in school — the star QB! That's quarterback in
8 case you came from another planet and didn't know. Every
9 girl in school would do anything to be in my shoes.
10 It's so awesome. Well, mostly. At least the times we're
11 together are. Thing is, football takes up a lot more time than
12 I thought. Did you know they practice *every* day? And not
13 just an hour or so, but three or four! By the time practice is
14 over, he has to eat supper. Then, he has to do his
15 homework. Most nights it's too late for him to even call me.
16 And on game nights, I don't get to spend time with him.
17 Well, duh, 'cause he's out on the field, right? Well, even after
18 it's over, the coach makes him stay and watch the game
19 tape since he's not only QB, he's also TC. Team captain. All
20 the other guys get to go out and party with their girlfriends,
21 but not Ron! He's stuck with the coach and I'm stuck alone.
22 I figured I could suffer through football season and it
23 would all be worth it. Then, he tells me they do weight
24 training in the off season. Every day!
25 Geez. I might as well be single. Since I started dating
26 Ron, I've become a football widow!

# 52. Big Mouthed Bird

(Girl)

1     My brother thinks he's funny. A real comedian. He lives
2 for pulling pranks and telling stupid jokes. Many of my
3 unsuspecting friends have fallen prey to his underwear in
4 the freezer joke or his fake spiders in their sleeping bags.

5     But this time he has gone too far! No telling how long
6 he's been cooking this prank up. It must've taken months
7 of patience. The boy can't sit still long enough to do his
8 homework, but this he can do?

9     See, he taught our parrot to speak. Not an easy feat I've
10 been told. They make you think it's easy when you buy
11 those stupid birds, but it's really not. It takes a lot of time
12 and practice. You think Brad would've given up on such a
13 task. But no! He had a much grander scheme in mind than
14 just teaching Pretty Bird how to say the normal bird
15 chatter. Heaven forbid he just teach the thing to say "Polly
16 want a cracker."

17     He taught her sounds and phrases. Only he didn't tell us
18 until the night my first boyfriend *ever* came over. My new
19 boyfriend of only *one* week. I was already worried about him
20 meeting my family, who wouldn't be? Then, when we were
21 sitting around talking, all of a sudden Pretty Bird squawks
22 and says, "Patty likes to poot. Patty likes to poot." Then
23 that stupid bird made a horrible sound that could've easily
24 come from the bathroom. Who knew a bird could even make
25 a noise like that without lips!

26     You should've seen my boyfriend's face. Worst part was,
27 the stupid bird wouldn't stop talking! It's a good thing my
28 boyfriend knew it was a joke or that bird just might have
29 been our dinner!

# 53. Restart Button

(Guy)

1    Some people are not meant to operate computers.
2    They're just not. Take this guy in my computer class. The
3    teacher told us to press F-one on our keyboard and the guy
4    starts typing an F and then the one. Then he yells out,
5    "Mine isn't working." He does this at least six times a day
6    in class. He never *ever* stops to think it might be him and
7    not the computer that isn't working, especially when no one
8    else in class ever had any problems with their computers.
9    But it got me thinking: What if everything on the
10   computer *was* that literal.? Like the restart button or the
11   backspace. Like you could just push them and be able to
12   undo or redo something you've done in your life.
13   That would be awesome, wouldn't it? Like your very own
14   time machine. It's not like you'd want to restart your whole
15   life. Who wants to go back to the days of drooling and diaper
16   rash, right? But specific things that you'd like to push a
17   button and undo. Like that time I asked Claire out in front
18   of everyone and she totally shot me down. Man, that was
19   embarrassing.
20   Or the time my mom came to band practice to pick me
21   up and she had a head of aluminum foil because she was
22   highlighting her hair.
23   Or, I know, the time I thought it'd be funny to stick my
24   tongue on the metal pole outside the school when it was
25   twenty degrees outside. Those would definitely be restart
26   moments.
27   Think about it. What would be yours?

# 54. It Can't Be Happening

(Girl)

1     Oh my gosh. It's happening. It really is. You hear about
2  things like this all the time. You see it in other people.
3  Maybe you even point and laugh and say stupid things like,
4  "Isn't that cute?" And then wham! You look in the mirror
5  and it's *you!* And then, let me tell you, it's *not* cute. Or
6  funny. Not funny at all!

7     It's so unexpected. I'm too young! My whole life is in
8  front of me. I can't start down this path now, or who knows
9  where I'll end up. Well, I guess I *know* where I'll end up. I
10  don't have to look too far to figure that one out!

11     Odd how it started out so small. So inconspicuously.
12  Little things I said or did. A gesture with my hand that
13  seemed all too familiar. And then, out of what seemed like
14  nowhere, there I was singing an oldies song at the top of my
15  lungs ... *just like my mother!* I didn't even flinch. Knew every
16  word. Even sang to the instrumental part. Who does that?!
17  I'll tell you who — my mother! I'm morphing into her. Just
18  like everyone says. Pretty soon I'll be saying things like,
19  "Because I said so." Or, "Turn that TV down!"

20     Then it won't be long before I'll be going to bed early and
21  eating only salad for dinner and never eating a candy bar
22  because "it goes straight to my hips!" I'll be *old* and no fun!
23  And people will say stupid things like, "Is that your sister?"
24  when they see my mother and me. And we'll finish each
25  other's sentences. And we'll wear our hair the same way.
26  And we'll read the same old boring magazine that tells you
27  how to decorate your house or cook healthy dinners and
28  doesn't care one iota about fashion or makeup ... or boys!

1    Oh my gosh! This is *so unfair!* I want my own life. I want to
2    be *me!* I don't want to be *her!*

# 55. Who's the Hippie?

(Girl)

1   My friend has become a total whack job. Like major off
2   the deep end. If I didn't know her better, I'd swear she's
3   doing drugs or something! I barely recognized her when I
4   saw her at the locker. In fact, I was just about to be rude
5   and tell her to get out of my friend's locker and then she
6   turned around.
7   I don't even know how or why this happened! She used
8   to be the most normal, conservative person I know, and
9   then overnight she's gone totally liberal! Like a chick from
10  the sixties or something. I'm serious. The girl is wearing tie-
11  dye! And braids, and gold tacky jewelry with the biggest
12  hoop earrings I've ever seen. And get this: She's sewn
13  flowers all over her jeans. *Flowers!* To top it off, she is
14  actually wearing some kind of beaded thing across her
15  forehead. Who knows where she could even find this kind of
16  stuff? I don't think Goodwill carries stuff *this* out of fashion!
17  If that's not bad enough, she's walking the halls
18  throwing out the peace sign like an actress in a bad sitcom.
19  I even overheard her say groovy to someone. *Groovy!* I keep
20  looking around to make sure I haven't fallen into a time
21  machine or something. But everyone else seems normal.
22  Well, as normal as they usually are. Which isn't saying
23  much. I mean, seriously, if you can stand out as a freak in
24  *this* crowd, there's got to be something really strange about
25  you.
26  Next thing I know, she'll be trading her cool convertible
27  in for a Beetle! Or, oh my gosh, one of those horrible, tacky,
28  carpeted *vans!* You know what I mean, the kind with flowers

1   and hearts and peace signs all over it. I don't know how this

2   happened, but someone's turned my friend into a *hippie!*

# 56. Is This All We're Gonna Do?

(Girl)

1     Let me tell you something: Parents are liars. They'll tell
2 you anything and you'll believe them because hello, they're
3 your parents. So of course I believed mine when they told
4 me we were going out for a day of family fun. They talked
5 things up. I was actually psyched to go with them. But you
6 know what my parents' idea of family fun is? Nothing but a
7 glorified walk through the woods! They call it hiking — I call
8 it *lame* with a capital L.
9     Seriously, it's nothing but walking through the woods. I
10 know you'll think I'm stupid, but I had no idea that's what
11 hiking actually was. I pictured cliffs and danger and rock
12 climbing. We were on a concrete path half the time! Then we
13 were on a dirt path that was so beat down it might as well
14 have been paved. No sense of adventure. No sense of
15 danger. And we didn't even see a single animal. Not even a
16 squirrel for Pete's sake! I can see more wildlife in my
17 backyard.
18     In fact, there wasn't one thing interesting about the
19 "hike." No interesting flowers. No mysterious ancient
20 markings. Nothing. Not even a creepy bug. Seriously. Not
21 even one spider and I see those in my house all the time.
22 Let me tell you, it was about as exciting as watching paint
23 dry. In fact, I think I had more fun watching the paint dry on
24 my walls last year when Mom painted my room than I did on
25 this family fun hike!
26     Well my parents can get "back to nature" all they want
27 on their own now. They won't sucker me into a glorified walk
28 again like that unless it leads to a mall! What a complete

1  and total waste of my day. I would've rather been studying
2  and believe me, that's saying *a lot!*

# 57. Squirrely Brother

(Girl)

1  Either my brother knows something I don't, or he's
2  totally lost his mind. He's acting like the end of the world is
3  coming or something. Yesterday, I went to the garage to
4  grab a box of my sweaters, and when I opened it up, I found
5  a box of cookies. I checked another box, and there were
6  three bags of pretzels and a box of donuts.
7      Why in the world would he be hoarding food like a
8  squirrel hiding food for hibernation? It's not like we're poor
9  or anything. I'm pretty sure he's never gone hungry a day in
10 his spoiled little life. And as far as I know, Mom hasn't put
11 a ban on junk food or anything. And it's not like I want his
12 stupid cookies or donuts. I haven't eaten stuff like that
13 since I made the volleyball team. The coach goes crazy over
14 athletes eating junk food. So why the heck is my brother
15 acting like a food freak? Paranoia? Why is the end of the
16 world or alien abduction kind of sci-fi crud filling his pathetic
17 little brain?
18     When I confronted him about it, he said it was no big
19 deal and none of my business. He even shoved me out of his
20 room and told me to stop being his mother. Well, all I know
21 is he's going to be very surprised when he goes to get his
22 stash the next time. I may not eat junk like that, but my
23 boyfriend sure does! That'll teach my squirrely little brother.

# 58. I'm a Failure and a Liar
## (Guy)

1     "Oh what a tangled web we weave, when first we
2 practice to deceive." Sir Walter Scott sure knew what he
3 was talking about. I've started a web so big and so
4 complicated, it's about to suffocate me.
5     I don't even know why I lied. I wouldn't have been the
6 first or the last person to fail the driving test. It's practically
7 a running joke around here that the only ones who pass the
8 first time around are the really hot girls. When someone
9 asked me about my test I could have easily joked that the
10 theory still stands.
11     I could have ... but I didn't. How could I? Me and my
12 stupid mouth told everyone how I was going to ace the
13 stupid thing. That I would be the one teaching the tester guy
14 a thing or two about driving. He'd be asking me for tips by
15 the time the test was through. My father is a race car driver
16 after all. It's in my blood. Blah. Blah. Blah.
17     Oh, I laid it on thick. There was no way I could come
18 back to school and admit that not only did I fail the darn
19 test, the dude wouldn't even let me *finish* the course! Said
20 I was a danger to anyone on the road and I needed to log
21 some serious supervised driving time. Now how many
22 people has *that* happened to?
23     So of course everyone wanted to see my license when I
24 got back to school. So I had to lie. Told them my mom was
25 so proud she took it to make copies to send to all the family.
26 Then the next day they wanted me to drive them home from
27 school. Another lie. Now I've been designated to drive on
28 prom night since my parents have the biggest ride and it's

only two days away! No time for me to retest. Even if I could pass this time around, I don't have time to do it.

Do you know the lie I've had to make up? Well, let me just put it this way, I now have to miss my own prom because my aunt's cousin's daughter who is blind and missing a leg needs a date to her prom in another county on the *same exact night,* and so my mother volunteered me to take her. How could I possibly say no to that?

# 59. Bucktooth Becky? I Wish!

(Girl)

1     I am so sick of people asking me when I'm finally going
2 to lose my baby teeth. They think they're so funny with their
3 little tooth fairy jokes and stuff. Last year I had at least
4 twenty quarters shoved in the slots of my locker. And
5 sometimes I get notes from the "tooth fairy" stuck in my
6 books. And one time I had a box of Chiclets gum on my desk
7 with a sticky note that said, "Use these until your big teeth
8 come in." Real funny stuff, I tell you.

9     It's not like I don't understand why — look at these
10 choppers. Are these not the tiniest adult teeth you've ever
11 seen? But they *are* adult teeth. My baby teeth were even
12 smaller if you can believe that!

13     What I wouldn't give for a big honking set of teeth. I
14 wouldn't even care if they called me Bucktooth Becky! It's
15 got to be better than Little Baby Becky! I'm sixteen and my
16 smile could belong on a six-year-old! Or probably even
17 younger! Don't you get big teeth when you're like two or
18 something? Why are my stinking teeth so dang small?
19 Nothing else on me is out of proportion.

20     My ears are normal. Nose is normal — maybe even a hair
21 big. Eyes are normal. So what the heck's up with my teeth?
22 Did my mom not give me enough milk when I was little? Did
23 I miss some vital nutrient by being bottle fed instead of
24 nursed like all my cousins? Their teeth are all just fine!

25     All I know is I can't wait until I'm old enough to get
26 dentures. I'm getting the biggest set of chops they make!

# 60. Frozen Stiff

(Girl)

1     You always think you'll know what to do in a crisis
2 situation. You see yourself kneeing an attacker in the groin
3 or doing some swift karate chop to the neck. Maybe even
4 poking someone's eyes out. You think you'll be clearheaded
5 and calm no matter what life throws at you. Well, *wrong*.
6     There I was waiting on my friend to meet me at the mall.
7 I was a few minutes early so I was sitting in my car texting
8 some other friends, flipping stations on the radio. The
9 normal stuff. Then all of a sudden there's a guy at my
10 passenger side window.
11     Now here's the part I never *ever* thought I'd do. Who
12 would, right? I actually rolled down the window — only a few
13 inches in my moronic defense — to see what he wants and
14 the guy actually reaches in and starts yanking on my purse!
15 Only it's too big to fit through the window.
16     For a minute, I just sat there. Completely dazed by what
17 was happening. I couldn't have moved if I had to. Then,
18 when I finally realized what was going on, I started rolling up
19 my window with his arm still in my car. Unfortunately, I
20 wasn't fast enough. He got free and was running through the
21 parking lot — scot-free before I even thought to call nine-
22 one-one.
23     I couldn't believe it. So many things I could've done: *not*
24 rolled down my window, honked the horn like crazy, driven
25 off, called nine-one-one, screamed bloody murder. I did *none*
26 of them!
27     This week I enrolled in a self-defense class. Next time, I
28 won't freeze. I'll be ready.

# 61. Skirt Season — Ahhhh!

(Girl)

1  You know what my favorite season is? Winter. Want to
2  know why? 'Cause when else can you wear pants every day
3  and nobody cares? Even at school they allow us to switch
4  from our khaki skirts to khaki pants. It's pure heaven.
5      But guess what's coming up? The worst season of all:
6  *skirt* season. That means I have to find a razor sharp enough
7  to mow down the forest I've been growing on my legs. And
8  keep up all that maintenance! Do you know how many
9  minutes that adds to my shower time? I used to be able to
10 get up at seven-fifteen and be out the door by seven-thirty
11 — shower, breakfast, and all! Now, I'll have to get up at
12 least a half hour earlier so I'll have time to keep the
13 stubblies under control. My leg hair grows back darker and
14 faster than any man's facial hair. They get five o'clock
15 stubble — I get it by eleven a.m.!
16     That's not even the worst of it. My legs have this
17 wonderful knock-kneed look to them. Instead of going out in
18 a normal way, my legs seem to bow inward. Not a great
19 look, believe me.
20     And once I clear away the stubble you get to really see
21 the skin beneath. And that is *not* a good thing. See, bugs
22 seem to love me. Five minutes outside on a spring night and
23 I've got a good hundred bug bites up and down my legs. Now
24 the fresh ones are bad enough — red and sometimes oozy.
25 But I've got hundreds of scars dotting my legs as well.
26 Beautiful, I tell you.
27     But if that's not enough to make you want to vomit, look
28 at these things! But wait, make sure you put on your

1    sunglasses 'cause these babies will blind you. They don't
2    come any whiter than this.
3       I think there's really only one place for a girl like me to
4    live — Alaska!

# 62. I Am Not Sulking!

## (Guy)

1     Quit staring at me. I'm fine. You don't need to call the
2  doctor, my teacher, the police, a minister, or heaven forbid,
3  Grandma. There's nothing to talk about. Nothing to confess
4  to. Nothing to work out. There's just nothing.
5     Sometimes I just don't feel like talking. Why can't you
6  get that? Why can't you leave me alone? Seriously. Quit.
7  Staring. At. Me.
8     I am *not* doing drugs. I am *not* pouting. I am *not* sulking.
9  I am *not* planning ways to sneak out, steal the car, or drink
10  myself into oblivion. I am just sitting. Doing nothing.
11  *Nothing.*
12     You don't need to check my pupils. I don't need therapy
13  or medication. Or an art class to teach me the value of
14  expression. I just want to be left alone. It's not a crime. It's
15  not abnormal. It's nothing you need to worry about, read a
16  book about, or write in your journal about.
17     Just because you like noise all the time, doesn't mean I
18  have to. Quiet is nice. Believe me. It doesn't make me a
19  freak, or an introvert, or even a troubled teen. I just like to
20  sit and stare into space and let my mind go free. What is
21  wrong with that?
22     *(Pause)* Seriously. You're creeping me out. Stop
23  analyzing me. I am not high, buzzed, stoned, or tripping. I
24  just don't feel like talking. *(Pause and stare.)*
25     OK, fine. You win. Look, I'm taking out my cell phone.
26  I'm dialing a friend. I'm going to talk on the phone about
27  stupid things that nobody cares about. Will that make you
28  happy?

# 63. Bad Picker
(Guy)

1     It's gotten to the point that I *hate* going out with my
2  girlfriend. And not for the normal reasons either. Like it
3  costs too much. Or it takes time away from my friends. Or
4  even that it takes time away from my gaming. Or even the
5  fact that I have to wear nicer clothes that I have to iron.

6     Normally I love being with her. She's pretty. She's funny.
7  When we're just hanging out, everything is great. But
8  declare the night a date and all of a sudden her expectations
9  go sky high and nothing seems to go right.

10    The fact is they all start out the same. And basically
11  they all *end* up the same, too. With her looking like I'm the
12  biggest moron on the face of the earth. How can a simple
13  question "What do you want to do?" cause me so much
14  agony?

15    I try to be a gentleman. I *try* to let her pick. Heck, I've
16  even tried forcing her to pick. Never works. We go back and
17  forth with, "What do *you* want to do?" "I don't care. What
18  do *you* want to do?" You know, the convo that can virtually
19  last forever. I eventually end up picking and she ends up
20  looking disappointed.

21    I can never seem to pick the right thing. I've tried the
22  movies, bowling, fancy dinner, the works. I even tried
23  bringing her to that place in the mall where you build your
24  own stuffed animal. Thinking she would find that romantic.
25  She didn't. She thought it was childish.

26    So why won't she pick something in the first place if I
27  can never get it right? It's driving me crazy. I'm not a mind
28  reader. I have no clue what a girl wants — why can't she
29  make it easier for both of us and just *tell me!*

# 64. Makeover Winner

(Girl)

1   When I got the call, I was so excited. I was going to be
2   in a magazine! A real, on-the-shelf-in-every-major-store
3   kind of magazine. Everyone would see my face. All the kids
4   in my school. All the guys that never asked me out. And
5   especially the ones that did and then broke my heart!
6   They'd see the new, awesome me and the guys would be
7   jealous and the girls would be full of envy.
8       That's right. I won a spot for February's Makeover of the
9   Month! Three whole pages would be dedicated to me and all
10  the wonderful things they would be doing to me. New
11  clothes, new hair, new makeup. Voilá! New person!
12      But then reality hit me. Not only would they see the new
13  and improved, ultra made up and *gorgeous* me, they'd see
14  the *before* picture. The horrible, no makeup allowed, wearing
15  sweats and a T-shirt picture with my hair frizzed out and
16  unstraightened *before* picture! The one I sent that made me
17  look as bad as humanly possible. The one that was
18  supposed to show them how desperately I needed to win the
19  Makeover of the Month contest. The one I took after not
20  sleeping for two days so the bags under my eyes would be
21  as dark as my unwashed hair. Oh, and did I mention that I
22  hadn't plucked my eyebrows for *three* weeks before I took
23  that picture?! Or that I purposely ate chocolate to make my
24  face break out?
25      That picture's going to be the kiss of death! No one will
26  ask me out after that gets published. It won't matter how
27  great I look in the *after* picture, the *before* one is going to make
28  me the laughingstock of the school. I don't think Makeover of
29  the Month is worth it. I'm calling those people back.

# 65. My Bank Hates Me
(Girl)

1    My bank is out to get me. They tell me I have this
2  courtesy thing where they'll pay even if I don't have the money
3  in my account, which sounds like a pretty great thing to me.
4  And then when I'm actually short a few dollars, they charge
5  me thirty bucks! How can they even do that? The debit for my
6  lunch was only six dollars and twenty-two cents. Now I'm
7  going to pay thirty-six for it? Isn't that against the law or
8  something? They're like a bunch of loan sharks!

9    Worst thing is, that was last week. This week I wrote
10 something in my checkbook wrong and I bounced *five* items!
11 That's *five* of those stupid thirty-dollar fees! And if you can't
12 do math that quickly, let me fill you in — that's *one-hundred*
13 *and fifty dollars in fees!* I can't afford that! I can barely afford
14 the transactions — *obviously.* So how do they expect me to
15 pay those kind of fees?! It's like they're out to get me. I
16 make *one* tiny mistake in my math and now I'm sunk
17 forever? I'll never get out of this hole.

18   I told them it would be better if they just didn't *pay* at
19 all. Just let the machine tell me I don't have any money.
20 Wouldn't that be easier and smarter for all of us? Besides,
21 they can't expect me to know exactly how much money I
22 have at all times. I'm a student, not an accountant! Who has
23 time to keep up with receipts all the time? I'm lucky if I
24 remember to write in the checkbook half the things I buy.

25   I guess my grandma had the right idea after all — she
26 kept her money in a coffee can and paid cash for everything.
27 With these ridiculous fees, I don't think my bank has left me
28 any choice!

# 66. Upstaged by Sister

(Girl)

1      So tonight was supposed to be *my* night. The big one.
2 After four years of studying my butt off, I had graduated
3 valedictorian of my class. My whole family had come to town
4 for the big celebration party that my mom and I had been
5 planning for weeks.

6      Everything was going great, too. Mom even let me have
7 a sip of wine when Dad made the toast about how excited
8 they were about my future and how they knew I was going
9 to do great things. Everyone in my family clapped and
10 smiled at me like I'd won the Nobel Peace Prize or
11 something.

12      And then my dearest sister Holly had to open her mouth.
13 She said she hated to steal the moment, but she had some
14 important news she wanted to share while the whole family
15 was gathered. Then *bam* — she stole the show. Out from
16 under the table comes a big shiny ring and Holly announces
17 she's getting married! *Married!*

18      How could she do that to me?! She knows there are two
19 things this family loves: marriages and babies! I half
20 expected her to announce she was pregnant, too, just to
21 seal the deal even more. But she didn't really need to.
22 Immediately all eyes were off me and onto Holly. All the
23 usual exclamations of surprise and then the inundation of
24 questions: Where? When? How did he propose? What colors
25 would she use? Was I going to be her maid of honor? Believe
26 me, I was *all* ready to answer that one with a big fat *no,* but
27 someone cut me off before I could.

28      Next thing I know, the same glasses that just a few

1 minutes ago were raised in my honor, were now being raised
2 even higher for Holly. Like getting engaged is such a big
3 accomplishment!
4     She did this to me on purpose! She could've waited until
5 tomorrow! She could've announced it at the airport if she
6 wanted. Just not tonight. All I know is the day of her
7 wedding, I'm going to announce that I'm pregnant! That'll
8 serve her right!

# 67. Never-Ending Hiccups
## (Guy)

1     I am never going to make it to college. I'll be the only
2  one in my family to work at a fast food restaurant for the
3  rest of my life. My parents' dreams for me, my dreams for
4  myself, are gone.
5     Another thing I am never going to do: get married.
6  That's because I am never going to have a girlfriend. Which
7  means I am never going to have a fiancée. Which of course
8  means that I am never going to have a wife.
9     You're probably thinking I'm the most pessimistic
10 person you've ever met and that a guy like me doesn't
11 *deserve* a college education or the experience of marriage. I
12 can understand why you might think that about me. But I
13 am not a negative thinker, a sad and lonely pessimist at
14 heart, I am a realist. I see the way things are and I accept
15 them. Well, I accept them only after I've tried everything I
16 possibly can think of to change them!
17    See, my problem is this: Every time I get nervous or
18 anxious, I get the hiccups. Actually, that is putting it lightly.
19 I get the most obnoxious never-ending hiccups you've ever
20 heard. Gut-wrenching noises that fill a room and shake my
21 entire body! They're extremely annoying to not only me, but
22 everyone around me.
23    When I go to the dentist, the doctor, or even the
24 ophthalmologist! When I take an exam or have to give a
25 presentation. When I ask someone out or if I am lucky
26 enough to go on a date, which is most likely set up prior to
27 meeting me. Those stupid hiccups show up. Every aspect of
28 my life is affected by these uncontrollable hiccups.

1    I've tried peanut butter, drinking from the other side of
2    the glass upside-down, standing on my head, swigging
3    cough medicine, and of course, holding my breath. Nothing
4    works. Once they get started they take forever to stop. Can
5    you see that at a wedding? That whole "repeat after me"
6    thing would be a nightmare! I couldn't finish any section of
7    the ACT exam because who can read when their head is
8    convulsing?!
9        So that's why I say *(Hiccup)* that I *(Hiccup)* am never
10   going to *(Hiccup)* — oh, forget it! I think, *(Hiccup)* you get the
11   *(Hiccup)* picture!

# 68. Stuck Like Glue
# to Her Beau

(Girl)

1   My best friend has got to be the most emotionally
2   dependent person I've ever met. You know how they also call
3   plastic wrap cling wrap? Well, that's her.

4   But this latest thing is the worst! We had the whole day
5   planned out. Heather, Kristina, and I were going to go prom
6   dress shopping and then out to dinner. A total girl fest.
7   Clearly there was no need to specify that *no* boys would be
8   allowed. Right?!

9   Well, wrong, apparently. We meet at the mall and guess
10  who shows up with her boyfriend? Heather, of course! Like
11  she can't go a whole five hours or so without him! We try to
12  tell her that typically the guy doesn't see the prom dress
13  until the night he picks her up and you know what she says?
14  "Then how will he know what color corsage to get me? Or
15  what color tux to get?"

16  Seriously? Does the guy not understand colors? Can you
17  not just say red or blue and he'll get the picture? I'm
18  thinking that he probably learned his colors in kindergarten.

19  We thought we were doomed to spending the day with
20  him when I remembered a very important thing about my
21  best friend: She's even more superstitious than she is
22  clingy.

23  "Ah, that's too bad," I said to her as we started walking
24  off, the four of us.

25  "What is?" she asked.

26  "This thing I heard about proms being a lot like
27  weddings."

28  "What do you mean?" I could tell I had her attention

1  now. Heather loves anything and everything to do with
2  weddings. She'd been planning hers since the day she
3  turned five.

4     "You know how it's bad luck for the groom to see the
5  bride's dress? I heard it's the same thing with prom
6  dresses. Almost eighty percent of couples break up after
7  prom if the boyfriend saw their dress before the big night."

8     You should've seen her face. That's all it took. A few
9  minutes later it was just the way it should be — just us
10 girls!

# 69. Not Such a Tough Guy

(Guy)

1     When you're the quarterback of your school's football
2 team there are some things you should never ever do. Like
3 kiss your mom in public, or cry at a sad movie, or admit you
4 rented a chick flick with your girlfriend. But the number one
5 thing you should *never* do is write a heartfelt poem about
6 your feelings. *Ever.*
7     Even if it means you have to take a zero in a class you're
8 already borderline C in. I thought, "What could be the
9 harm?" I did the assignment. The teacher would read it. No
10 one would ever know.
11     Wrong. My teacher decides, without asking, to share a
12 student's poem out loud to the class. Oh, she didn't give my
13 name or anything. She didn't have to! Everyone knew it was
14 mine. Who else lost a parent when they were in elementary
15 school? It was so embarrassing! Especially when I started
16 crying — well, come on, you would have, too!
17     No one is going to respect me now. The team's going to
18 think I'm some emotional crybaby who can't be counted on.
19 They'll probably beat me up the next time I step foot in the
20 locker room. Who could blame them? Football players don't
21 cry in class. If anything we make other people cry in class!
22     What happened to student-teacher confidentiality?
23 Shouldn't she get fired or something? Where are my rights?
24 If I'd known she was going to read it out loud I never would
25 have written it! I'd take an F over this any day. I might as
26 well kiss football good-bye and join the band.

# 70. Not a Senior Skipper

(Guy)

1    Look, I know it's lame. In fact, it's probably pathetic at
2    best. But I don't care. A record is a record and I've worked
3    hard to get this one. There were so many days I could've
4    just thrown in the towel. Given in to the desire to stay home
5    and let the all-time record go. At least if I had given in to
6    illness, the loss wouldn't have been self-imposed.

7    But now? You want me to throw it all away? Throw in the
8    proverbial towel? Skip school and give up my record of never
9    having missed a day in the entire twelve years? Just
10   because some random people got together and dubbed it
11   Senior Skip Day? Just so I can go to the mall or the movies
12   or the water park with a bunch of other skippers?

13   The whole thing is really ridiculous. It's not like we're
14   staging a protest or anything. Yet everyone is acting like
15   we're waging war against the school. That if you don't skip,
16   you'll make everyone else look bad. "What can they do if we
17   *all* do it?" they say to me.

18   I'm going to guess the same thing they can do if only
19   *half* the kids do it. The teachers have already gotten wind of
20   it. I have a quiz or a project due in almost every class now.
21   Am I just supposed to forfeit my four-point-oh, too? Just so
22   I can be one of *them?* Those rebels?

23   Well my record might be lame to everyone else, but you
24   know what? It may be the only one I ever get! They've
25   already interviewed me for the local paper. I'm like the only
26   kid to have perfect attendance for all twelve years since
27   Adam Frolly did it fifteen years ago. I'm not throwing it all
28   away now! If the flu couldn't keep me home back in middle
29   school, Senior Skip Day is not going to faze me!

# 71. Too Healthy for a Sick Day
## (Guy)

1  So why do they give you sick days if you're not allowed
2  to use them? Sure I understand the concept that they are
3  for when you are sick. But what if you're like me? I never get
4  sick! I'm piling up a bunch of sick time I'll never get to use.

5  How is that fair? There's this one girl at work that
6  misses almost two or three times a month. We've even
7  nicknamed Migraine Monday after her. I'm totally missing
8  out because I'm healthy!

9  I thought I could just take a sick day if I wanted to. You
10  know, a mental health day or something. A day to rest and
11  de-stress. Who are they to deny me that?

12  So I took one. Called in sick and then spent the day with
13  my friend who I never get to see because I'm always
14  working. We had a blast, too. Went to lunch and then a
15  movie. Totally awesome.

16  I didn't even think to tell Eli not to post the pictures of
17  us on the Internet. I guess because I didn't think I was doing
18  anything wrong. I earned that sick day. I should be able to
19  use it, right?

20  So I go to work the next day and my boss fires me! Me
21  — the guy who never misses work. Me — the guy who has
22  only taken *one* sick day in a year and a half! He said I had
23  abused the policy by taking a sick day when I wasn't sick.
24  He even had the photos of me and Eli printed.

25  Funny that I don't see anyone going to Migraine Mary's
26  house to see if she's really got a headache or not!

27  I swear, sick days are a rip-off for healthy people like me!

# 72. Big Mouthed Father
### (Guy)

1      Sometimes my father is so dense. He walks right into a
2 land mine and doesn't even know it. Like last night, for
3 instance. My mom asks him, "How do you like my haircut?"
4 She's thrown it out there — the hand grenade with the pin
5 pulled. What does my clueless father say? "I can't even tell
6 you got it cut."
7      Kaboom! Proverbial body parts fill the room.
8      Even I know you don't tell someone who just spent a
9 hundred and thirty-five dollars to get her hair washed, cut,
10 and colored that she basically just threw that money away.
11 But whatever, right? Let my dad fend for himself. Suffer the
12 consequences of his foot in his mouth. And I would, except
13 now it's affecting me!
14      We had just sat down to dinner. Mom was already
15 steaming over the whole haircut thing. She puts a premade
16 frozen, but now cooked, lasagna on the table. Want to know
17 what my brilliant father asks? "You didn't make the
18 lasagna?"
19      My mom looks confused. Honestly, I am, too. We all just
20 saw her take it out of the oven. Of course she made the
21 lasagna. Who else did he think made it?
22      Then realization hits. "Oh, you mean did I spend two
23 hours in the kitchen making homemade sauce and dirtying
24 up six pans to make homemade lasagna?"
25      Luckily, my father knows the bomb is in the air. He
26 doesn't answer.
27      "No. I. Did. Not. *Make.* The. Lasagna." She spits out at
28 him. "I was too busy getting my *hair done!*"

1      Then she took the lasagna and dumped it in the trash.

2      *Kaboom!* The bomb went off as she left the room in a

3  huff.

4      I'm pretty sure we won't be getting homemade *anything*

5  for a while.

# 73. Not Hard to Please

(Girl)

1    I don't think I'm hard to please. I'm not really picky or
2  snobbish about clothes, shoes, jewelry, or anything. You
3  can buy me just about anything and I'll be thrilled with it.
4  My mom tells everyone that you can give me a sticker and
5  I'll smile all day. That's how easy I am to please.

6    I have proof, too. One year for Christmas I got a ski
7  jacket as my "big" present. Not even sure why since I've
8  never skied a day in my life. And I hate the cold so I spend
9  as little time in it as possible. But to make matters worse,
10 this jacket had zip off sleeves so that the coat could
11 become a vest. Without the blue sleeves, the white puffy
12 vest would make me look like a snowman.

13    But did I complain? No. I actually ended up liking that
14 stupid vest-coat because it was the warmest coat I've ever
15 had. Did I mention how much I *hate* the cold? Now most
16 girls would have thrown a fit over getting something like that
17 for Christmas. Not me. Like I said, I'm easy to please.

18    So why then would my boyfriend have such a hard time
19 figuring out what to get me for my birthday? He could have
20 bought me almost *anything* and I would've been happy.

21    *Almost* anything. Know what he gets me? A bowling ball.
22 With my initials engraved in it. Now that could've been
23 sweet *if* our first date, or *any* of our dates, had been to a
24 bowling alley. But not once have he and I ever stepped foot
25 in one. Together or separately!

26    I thought maybe he had plans for us to start bowling
27 together. He didn't. When I asked why he got me a bowling
28 ball, he said, "Because I knew you didn't have one."

1    Really? *Really?!* Out of all the things I *don't* have, he
2  thought I needed that? I *don't* have diamond earrings. I *don't*
3  have a cashmere sweater. I *don't* have a puppy or a kitten!
4    Why didn't he buy me something like that?!

# 74. Nosey Neighbor

(Girl)

1     My neighbor is such a busybody. She is *always* sticking
2 her nose into my business. Whenever she sees cars in front
3 of my house after school, she calls my mother at work to
4 see if she knows I'm throwing a party. Which I'm not! A few
5 friends is *not* a party, Mrs. Miller!

6     Mom says to just ignore her. She's old and harmless.
7 My mother pacifies her every time she calls. But I can't just
8 ignore her. I feel like I'm being spied on twenty-four-seven. I
9 don't doubt for a minute that that old lady's got a pair of
10 binoculars glued to her face.

11     When I come home from a date, she's out the door in
12 thirty seconds flat. Turning on her porch light. Taking out the
13 trash. Bringing her dog out. One time she even started
14 pruning her bushes, in the dark, just so she could spy on me!

15     And she talks, too. "You sure wouldn't see this back in
16 *my* day," she'll say. "A boy and girl all alone out on the
17 porch." That's probably because they didn't even have
18 porches back in *her* day!

19     If you ignore her, she just gets louder. "Some people
20 might get the *wrong* idea about a girl like that."

21     A girl like what? A normal teenage girl trying to get a
22 simple kiss goodnight? What's so wrong about that?

23     One time we were in the car kissing goodnight and she
24 actually turned a flashlight on us. "Oh, I thought you were
25 robbers," she said.

26     Yeah, 'cause robbers always sit in your driveway with the
27 car running and the lights on! I'm surprised she didn't call
28 the police just to embarrass me even more. How can Mom
29 say that she's harmless? She's ruining my life!

# 75. Dream on, Mom!

(Girl)

1    I finally understand what's been going on with my
2  mother. She's been acting so strange lately. All the time
3  asking me if I like the shirt she's wearing or if I want to
4  borrow something out of her closet.
5    I thought she'd lost her mind. What girl my age wants to
6  wear something of her mother's? She even offered to take
7  me shopping at her favorite store. Uh ... gee, thanks, Mom,
8  but no! I wouldn't be caught dead wearing something from
9  that old-lady store.
10    I figured maybe she was going through some sort of
11  identity crisis or something. That for some reason she
12  needed me to validate her or something weird like that. I
13  even thought that maybe she and Dad were getting a
14  divorce. Why else the sudden interest in her wearing clothes
15  I liked? She was trying to look hip or young again. Maybe
16  even a midlife crisis sort of thing. Then yesterday it all
17  clicked into place.
18    A couple of weeks ago I borrowed a pair of my mom's
19  jeans. Not just to wear, well, I did wear them, but only
20  because it was spirit week at school and for Wacky
21  Wednesday you were supposed to dress like a nerd.
22    I'd forgotten all about it until I was putting my clothes
23  away yesterday and there they were. Mom's jeans in my
24  basket. I figured she'd just put them in there by accident so
25  I brought them to her. But it was no mistake. She tried to
26  give them to me. "Oh, you keep them, honey," she said. "If
27  you like them so much, they're yours!"
28    I suppose I could've been nice and kept them. Never told

1  her the truth about why I wore them in the first place. But
2  sometimes you just can't help your gut reaction. The words,
3  "Dream on, Mom," were out of my mouth before I knew it. I
4  could tell I hurt her feelings, and I feel bad about that. But
5  seriously, me? In those *mom jeans?* Come on!

# 76. Tattoos Are Forever
(Guy)

1     I never really understood the big deal about tattoos.
2  Figured it's a personal choice that shouldn't matter to
3  anyone but the person getting it. I never saw me being the
4  one to fight with my parents about the right to express
5  myself artistically on my own body however I wanted.
6     And I probably never would have if it weren't for Missy.
7  Missy Monroe. My little M&M as I liked to call her because
8  she was so incredibly sweet. And hott, too! We'd been
9  dating almost a year when Missy jokingly said I should get
10  a tattoo of an M&M as a symbol of my love for her. At least
11  I thought she was joking. She certainly didn't have any
12  symbols of love for me permanently marked on her body. So
13  I laughed it off.
14     Two weeks before the big one-year anniversary date, she
15  brings it up again. Only this time she makes it clear she's
16  not joking. She totally expects me to get a tattoo as her
17  anniversary present. Not exactly the roses and perfume gift
18  I was planning on. So I tell her I can't afford a tattoo. They
19  are pretty expensive you know. Not a problem. She wants to
20  buy the tattoo for me as *my* anniversary present. I don't
21  even know what to say. Can't think of an excuse fast enough
22  to stop this thing in its tracks.
23     What choice did I have but to ask my parents? I still
24  wasn't sold on the idea of having a piece of candy
25  permanently inked on my forearm. So I didn't really go into
26  the discussion armed with a lot of reasons why they should
27  let me. But now here's the weird part: The minute they said
28  no, I knew I had to have it. Like all of a sudden I was dying

1  to have that tattoo. I fought with them every night until
2  finally they relented. I can be pretty persuasive when I want
3  to be. My mom even took me to get it.
4      So here it is. A big red M&M. It looks more like a blob
5  of ketchup or something. My permanent expression of love
6  for Missy Monroe. Who, by the way, I can't even stand,
7  because a week after our one-year anniversary, she broke up
8  with me to date my best friend. Want to know the worst
9  part? I don't even like M&Ms!

# 77. The "Right" Brother
## (Guy)

1      I am sick of living in my brother's shadow. Or rather,
2  him living in mine. The guy does *nothing* around here.
3  Nothing! While I am in the lab drawing up plans, welding
4  metal, testing theories, and all the other zillion things a
5  person has to do to try and get an object to fly, he's out
6  romancing the ladies. Or taking a nap because he's stayed
7  out too late. I've already been here for hours by the time he
8  shows up!

9      He's been living in my glory ever since the beginning. He
10  might not be here for the work, but the minute the press
11  shows up, he's there, front and center and smiling like a big
12  buffoon! Everyone thinks that just because we're brothers
13  he must be as brilliant as me.

14      Well, let me be quite clear on this: he's not. He's about
15  as bright as a hundred-year-old penny. He's got the common
16  sense of a child about to touch a hot stove. He's a complete
17  and utter moron. How could we have even come from the
18  same parents? I swear he has the IQ of a duck.

19      I can't tell you how many times he has almost gotten us
20  killed! I tell him to check something and he never does. Last
21  time we were airborne, he completely forgot our parachutes!
22  I can't count on him for anything.

23      I wish the papers would quit touting us as the "Wright
24  Brothers" because all of the success is due to *me!* Not him.
25  Not us! It should be the "Wright Brother" because the
26  r-i-g-h-t brother is *me!*

# 78. Obsessed with Texting

(Girl)

1     I did it. I broke the family record. My sister used to think
2  she was so hot because she always had the record, but in
3  her face! I had fourteen-thousand-two-hundred and twelve
4  texts last month. Over fourteen-thousand! I figured out that
5  I must have texted once a minute for every hour I was awake
6  last month. That is so awesome!
7     My parents can't say anything either because we have
8  unlimited texts. It doesn't cost them a penny more for me
9  to have so many. I even think they might have been
10 impressed that I could text so much in just thirty days. I
11 more than doubled my sister's record!
12    Do you know how often I have to clean out my inbox
13 because it gets too full? Every half hour! It's so crazy. None
14 of my friends even came close to that many. I should be like
15 a texting spokesmodel or something. Maybe the cell phone
16 company will hire me.
17    There is only one bad thing about it. My phone keeps
18 messing up now. My mom says it's because they don't
19 make phones that durable to do so many texts month after
20 month. She thinks I've worn it out, and I've only had it six
21 months! Surely a phone should last longer than that!? But
22 because of the whole fourteen thousand text thing, my
23 parents won't get me a new one. They think I *broke* it. How
24 is it fair that I have to pay for a defective product? The terms
25 are unlimited texts so the company should expect *unlimited*
26 *texts*. Which means the phone should be able to handle *any*
27 amount. Right? It seems unfair to punish me for bad quality
28 on their part!

1    With my phone acting so weird, how am I ever going to
2    beat my record?!

# 79. Homecoming Hoedown
## (Girl)

1     My high school is so lame! This is just one more reason
2 my parents should have sent me to private school instead
3 of the worst school in the world. They don't have an ounce
4 of class in that place. You think I'm kidding, but I'm not. In
5 the four years I've been here it has gone from bad to
6 pathetic!
7     Freshman year they decide to enforce a dress code that
8 made us look like kindergarteners instead of high schoolers.
9 Khaki pants, collared shirts, no flip-flops, no jewelry, and no
10 facial hair. Now, being a girl that last part didn't affect me
11 too much, but I know guys that had waited years to finally
12 grow out of the peach fuzz stage and they completely took
13 that away from them.
14     Sophomore year it was declared girls are *not* allowed to
15 carry purses *at all*. Not even to the bathroom. For obvious
16 reasons, this is the stupidest rule they could possibly come
17 up with. Do they even care how embarrassing that is for a
18 girl during certain times of the month? It's completely
19 humiliating. You might as well wear a sign around your neck
20 announcing your cycle.
21     Then we have my junior year. Up until yesterday, I
22 thought it was the worst. Mid-year they decide to get rid of
23 the student parking lot. They quoted parking lot accident
24 statistics and drug and gang activity as the reasons behind
25 forcing all students to *ride the bus*. Or walk. Which wasn't
26 an option for me since I live almost ten miles from the
27 school. But believe me, I considered it.
28     But senior year actually takes the cake. I finally get

1 nominated for Homecoming Court and the administration
2 announces the theme: Homecoming Hoedown. They want to
3 bring the Homecoming Court in on hay wagons wearing
4 overalls, bandanas, the works! They probably want pieces of
5 straw hanging out of our mouths. Do you have any idea how
6 long I've dreamed of walking across the football field in a
7 semi-formal gown with a guy in a tux — not overalls?! Why
8 is everyone so bent on humiliating us?
9     I tell you what, this would not be happening in a *private*
10 school!

# 80. Model Mower

(Girl)

1    Oh my gosh! The guy next door could seriously be on
2  the cover of a magazine. He is *so* hott! I can't take my eyes
3  off him. It's gotten so bad that I've seriously become a
4  Peeping Tom. He goes out to mow the lawn and there I am,
5  glued to the window like some nosey old woman.
6      Who could blame me? The guy goes shirtless! And his
7  stomach is so ripped, it's better than a six-pack! It's like a
8  twelve-pack for sure. When he pushes the mower and those
9  forearm muscles bulge, I could melt into a puddle.
10    His skin is so tan — he's browner than a biscuit. At
11 least that's what my mother says. I've caught her staring at
12 him a couple of times, even though she tries to hide it. I
13 don't judge her. I'm the one that's obsessed with the guy.
14 I'm even starting to get depressed because summer is
15 almost over and what will happen then? It's not like he'll
16 shovel snow without his shirt on! How am I going to make
17 it through the whole winter without seeing *that?!* It makes
18 me want to cry just thinking about it. Why, oh why, couldn't
19 we live some place eternally warm! It's totally not fair.
20    Guess there's really only one thing to do — get video on
21 my phone! At least I can have that year-round. It won't be
22 the same, but it might get me through the tough times.
23 Man, I wish my phone had better zooming and higher quality
24 video. I wonder if I have time to get a new one before
25 summer ends?

# 81. Blonde Hero
(Girl)

1　　I've been blonde all my life so I've probably heard every
2　dumb blonde joke you can imagine. I've probably told a few
3　of them myself because to be honest, I really am *not* the
4　sharpest knife in the drawer when it comes to common
5　sense. Now, book smarts, I have them. Common sense, not
6　so much. But that's OK because the other day I proved that
7　even a dumb blonde like me can take charge of a situation
8　and become a hero.

9　　My friends and I had decided to have a last-day-of-
10　summer picnic. We have a great lake near my house so we
11　packed tons of food, found a great spot under a shady tree,
12　and were having a grand time. We barely even noticed this
13　old guy who was fishing not too far down from us.

14　　After a lot of talking and a lot of food, we were soaking
15　up the rays when we heard the old guy start yelling. When
16　we sat up, it didn't make sense what we saw. The guy's
17　head was barely above the water. In fact, when a wave would
18　come every few minutes, his head was submerged! We all
19　stood but didn't know what to do. Why wasn't he just
20　swimming to the shore? He wasn't that far out. Barely
21　twenty feet away from the bank.

22　　But clearly he was in trouble because he wasn't moving
23　and as another boat sped by out on the lake, the man was
24　submerged again. My friends and I took off running. I could
25　hear Teresa already yelling into her phone as we ran — she
26　was smart enough to dial nine-one-one the second she saw
27　what was happening, and she's blonde, too. By the time we
28　reached the edge, his face was out of water again, but

1  barely! I could see how scared and pale he was.

2      We motioned for him to swim to us, but he didn't move.

3  It was like he was glued there. At first I thought it was from
4  fear, and then I remembered seeing the guy before he got in
5  the water — dressed in a full set of waders! I figured
6  somehow the water had come up on him quickly and filled
7  his waders, practically cementing him to his spot. He was
8  obviously too scared to think straight, so I swam to him,
9  unhooked the straps, and pulled him out of his pants.

10    My friend Amanda — also a blonde — helped me drag
11  him to shore. A few minutes later the paramedics got there
12  and said we had saved his life. Three blonde heroes! Take
13  that you dumb blonde jokes!

# 82. Not Gonna Be Your Star

(Guy)

1     Let's just state the obvious and get it over with. I'm tall.
2 Very tall. In fact, I may very well be the tallest person you've
3 ever seen. I get it. I'm a freak. A giant. An Amazon sort of
4 guy. I've heard every joke ever made about being tall. They
5 don't even bother me. I guess after about a billion, you get
6 used to them.

7     You can quit trying to guess exactly how tall I am. I'll
8 just tell you: six feet, seven inches. Yeah. That's tall. And I
9 *know* that every other freakishly tall kid you've ever known
10 is a basketball player. But I am not. I repeat, *I do not play*
11 *basketball.*

12     I am so sick of every teacher, student, parent, or coach
13 asking me why I don't play on the high school team. They
14 make me feel guilty, like I don't have any school spirit
15 because I won't play ball. I am not being difficult. I swear. I
16 have as much school spirit as the next person.

17     Believe me, people, you do *not* want me on the team.
18 They are one hundred percent better off without me. I can't
19 even dribble. I swear. And I can't run to save my life. These
20 big feet trip me up all the time. Five seconds on the court
21 and I'd be flat on my face. And my hand-eye coordination is
22 the pits. I probably couldn't even catch the ball, much less
23 get it in the basket. I promise. I'm not trying to sabotage the
24 team, the school, my county, the state, or the country!

25     I'm just a really tall guy with no athletic talent. Yes, you
26 heard me correctly: height is *not* a talent!

# 83. Fender Bender
(Guy)

1     I am a felon. I am. I didn't mean to be. I just freaked
2  out. Who wouldn't? When you have only had your license for
3  three whole days, you do *not* want to be involved in an
4  accident. Especially with my dad. I knew if he found out that
5  I'd hit something, he'd never let me drive again.
6     And it was just a scratch. I swear! I really didn't even
7  know for sure if *I had* to turn it in. I figured the person would
8  just think a stray shopping cart hit their door or something.
9  In fact, I wasn't even sure I had actually hit the car. Maybe
10  a cart really had done it and there I was about to take the
11  blame for it.
12     Here's the thing though: If you're going to commit a
13  crime, which I swear I didn't really think I was, you should
14  not circle the parking lot two or three times while you decide
15  what you should do. Whoever called in the accident certainly
16  had every opportunity to write down my license plate
17  number, the make and model of my car, and probably a
18  personal description of me. Which just goes to show that I
19  was just confused. What other criminal hangs out at the
20  scene of the crime for so long?
21     In fact, by the time I got home I knew what I had to do.
22  I was going to call the police and turn myself in — I was! I
23  just had to wait for the right moment to tell my parents. I
24  figured it could wait until after dinner. I sure didn't want to
25  give my dad indigestion or anything.
26     But let me tell you one last thing. That little scratch on
27  that parked car would've been a whole lot easier to explain
28  if the police hadn't shown up at my door first!

# 84. Sister's Bodyguard

(Guy)

1     I can't believe my eyes. In fact, I really wish I could rip
2 my eyes right out of my head! This is the most disgusting
3 thing I've ever seen. She calls *this* dancing? If Mom and Dad
4 were here they would have a cow. Look at all the grinding
5 and mauling going on out there! And Brittany is right in the
6 middle of it. Why did I ever agree to keep an eye on her? No
7 brother should have to see his little sister dancing like that.
8     Why aren't the teachers or the parent chaperones doing
9 something about it? They're just standing around talking,
10 drinking punch, and ignoring the whole thing. What is wrong
11 with them? They sure didn't turn a blind eye on this kind of
12 behavior at my freshman dance. How could things have
13 changed so much in just three short years? You wait until I
14 tell Mom and Dad; they'll be enrolling her in private school
15 before the night is over!
16     *(Pause, look out)* Oh my gosh! What does she think she's
17 doing? Acting like that? It's embarrassing! Well, she can't
18 just expect me to stand by and do nothing. Look at her!
19 She's practically on the floor. I swear, I think she's taunting
20 me.
21     Oh, now that's really pushing it! Look at her boyfriend's
22 hand! Look where it is! He'd better move that baby up a few
23 inches. *(Pause)* Maybe I should just go out there and move
24 it for him. Yeah, I think maybe I should go out there and
25 teach him a thing or two about respecting my baby sister.

126

# 85. Rules for a Semi-Stalker
(Guy)

1     There are some things you should never do when
2 following the girl of your dreams around the school. One of
3 them is to never follow her into the bathroom. Believe me,
4 that is extremely frowned upon, even if you do it by
5 accident.

6     The second thing you should never do is follow her to her
7 class if that means you will be five minutes late to your own
8 class because *your* room is on the extreme opposite of the
9 school. That will get you a Saturday detention. Or two.

10     The third thing you should never do when following the
11 girl of your dreams is not pay attention to where you are
12 going because you are too focused on her. That will get you
13 a broken nose, six stitches, and a lecture from your mother
14 who will never believe you when you tell her the locker just
15 jumped out at you.

16     The last thing you should never *ever* do is follow her
17 around on Club Day at school and sign up for whatever she
18 signs up for just so you can be near her. This I know for a
19 fact because I am now the *only* guy signed up for a club
20 called Girls of Grace *and* the first ever Scrapbooking Club of
21 Henry High.

22     Oh, and I guess the very last thing you should never ever
23 do when following the girl of your dreams is let your current
24 girlfriend catch you following the girl of your dreams around
25 school. That will get you another broken nose, a few more
26 stitches, a lecture from your mom, and a Dear John letter.
27 And if you're really unlucky like me, she'll *tell* the girl of your
28 dreams and then you'll get one last thing: a restraining
29 order.

# 86. You're Wrong, Grandma

(Girl)

1      I think my grandma watches too much television. Well,
2  actually it's more specific than that. My grandma watches
3  too much *news*. She's become cynical and jaded. She's all
4  the time telling me, "See, Kara, that's what the world's
5  come to. Not a decent person left in it. 'Cept you and me
6  and Brother North." Brother North's our minister. He's one
7  person that could never do wrong in Grandma's eyes.

8      I have to admit, I was starting to buy into the whole
9  "world's gone to h-e-double-hockey sticks" thing. It doesn't
10 take too many minutes in front of the news to believe that
11 there are a whole lot of bad people in the world. Maybe even
12 makes you believe there are more of *them* than there are *us*.

13     That's why my flat tire the other day was the best thing
14 that ever happened to me. It completely restored my faith in
15 the human race. I was about ten miles from my house when
16 I felt my car start to thump on the right-hand side. When I
17 pulled over, my tire was practically shredded and I was
18 riding on the rim. I thought, "No problem. I've changed a tire
19 before." But when I got the tools out of my trunk, the socket
20 wouldn't fit the lug nuts on my wheel. I had no way to get
21 the tire off.

22     As I stood there staring at it — like that was going to
23 help — a guy in a truck stopped to offer help. I have to
24 admit, I was scared at first — all those scary news stories
25 can make you paranoid! I figured he was going to throw me
26 in his car and drive off. But he didn't and when his socket
27 wouldn't fit the lug nuts either, he said he'd go get one and
28 come back.

1     Now here's the really incredible part: while he was gone,
2     *ten* more people stopped to offer help to me. *Ten!* And I
3     wasn't even on a main road where there was a lot of traffic.
4     Now if *that* doesn't prove Grandma wrong, maybe this will:
5     it was only twenty degrees outside! No one in their right
6     mind stops to help someone in *that* kind of weather! So, you
7     see, there really are good people in the world, Grandma.

# 87. The Procrastinator

(Guy)

1  I am totally freaking out. It's two a.m. and look at me!
2  I'm hyped up on caffeine, my eyes are bugging out of my
3  head, and I still have five pages to write for this paper that's
4  due tomorrow. Why do I do this to myself?! The teacher told
5  us about this assignment three weeks ago. Twenty-seven
6  days ago and what do I do?! I wait until the night before to
7  actually do something about it. This paper counts for half
8  my grade for this period. Why, oh why, do I do this stupid
9  stuff?
10  I had good intentions. I did. The first week I went to the
11  library and checked out four books on the subject. But did
12  I even crack them open once since the day I brought them
13  home? No! They've been sitting on my dresser collecting
14  dust or getting buried under piles of clean clothes. I forgot I
15  even had them until I was digging out my track sweatshirt.
16  There must be something psychologically wrong with
17  me. No one would put themselves through this on purpose.
18  Seriously. Look at me! I am sweating from panic. My hands
19  are shaking and I think I'm going to faint! But do I have time
20  to faint? No! I have to figure out what I'm going to write
21  about and I have to do it *now!* No time to panic. No time to
22  sit and ponder. Or write and rewrite. I've got to get this right
23  the first time. No edits. No spelling errors. Perfect
24  punctuation. Excellent grammar. Well, who can do that, I
25  ask you?! No one! That's who!
26  Oh, what's the use? This paper is going to stink. I might
27  as well give up and go to bed. But next time I am starting
28  earlier. I swear!

# 88. Overenthusiastic
(Girl)

1  Why does my teacher hate me? Every paper I turn in is
2  covered in red. She says I should not use an exclamation
3  point after every sentence!
4  *(Mimics.)* "Exclamation points should be used sparingly.
5  Rarely, even."
6  But I say, "Why?! Why, Mrs. Tuttle?! If you believe in
7  what you're writing, why not be enthusiastic?! Why *not* be
8  passionate?! When did exuberance become a bad thing?!
9  When did excitement become something to be censored?!
10 That's just who I am! I get excited about things I believe in!
11 I am not afraid to show that I care! I'm not afraid to have
12 emotions!"
13 Why is she trying to change me?! Why does she want us
14 all to submit robotic emotionless papers with no heart, no
15 feeling?! Why is that better?! Why is that more acceptable?!
16 She wants me to rewrite the paper! She'll even give me
17 a better grade if I do! And all I have to do is remove the very
18 thing that makes me who I am! It's like a deal with the devil!
19 Selling my soul, my very passion, for an A!
20 Who is she?! The exclamation point police?! Just
21 because she is a dull, lifeless person doesn't mean we all
22 need to be! If we were colors, she'd be gray and I'd be
23 yellow! *Neon yellow!* And what's wrong with that, I ask
24 you?! Why is gray right and yellow wrong?! Well, I refuse to
25 conform! I refuse to let go of my passion! My zeal for life!
26 Mrs. Tuttle, I refuse to be gray!

# Section 2
# Duologues

# Out-of-Control Cop

(2 Guys)

## 1

89. TOM'S VERSION
2

3    So there I was cruising down the road, listening to this
4 new jazz CD my brother got me, and here come the red and
5 blue lights. The guy is flying down the road in my direction
6 and I'm sitting there calm as can be thinking, "Man, he's
7 really after someone!"
8    Turns out that someone was me! I didn't even pull over
9 at first because I was sure he was after someone else. I
10 knew I hadn't been speeding, but if I had it could barely
11 have been five miles over the limit. Definitely nothing to get
12 pulled over for!
13    Finally I pull off the side and as I'm getting out of the
14 car, he's slamming me into the side of it. "Put your hands
15 in the air," he screams at me, like I'm an escaped convict
16 or something. Of course I do what he says. I don't want any
17 trouble. I don't even know *why* I'm in trouble.
18    The cop starts patting me down like I'm going to be
19 packing heat and he's yelling at me the whole time. I can
20 hear cars whizzing past us and I'm not sure what scares me
21 more. Is this out-of-control cop going to shoot me or is a car
22 going to lose control and ram into me?
23    I try to ask him what I've done wrong but the minute I
24 open my mouth he starts shouting at me. "Don't get smart
25 with me, boy!" and "You open your mouth one more time
26 and I'm taking you to jail." One *more* time? I've only opened
27 it once! What is wrong with this guy? Does he have me
28 confused with some serial killer or something?

1    When he finally lets me go, he starts searching through
2  my car. I don't have anything to hide but I'm pretty sure he's
3  not supposed to be doing that without a warrant, but given
4  the fact that he's the one with the gun — and the obviously
5  really short temper — I don't say anything. Just let him dig
6  through the garbage and work clothes that are scattered all
7  over my car. He seems disappointed when he doesn't find
8  anything.
9    After about ten minutes, he gives up. He takes his
10 sunglasses off and looks me up and down. "I'll be watching
11 you, boy," he says, and then he gets in his car and speeds
12 off. It was all so unreal. Like something in a really bad
13 movie. In fact, it's so bizarre sometimes I think I must've
14 dreamt it!
15
16                 90. OFFICER MADD'S VERSION
17
18    Teenagers today are so out of control. I can't tell you
19 how many tickets I write in a day just to smart aleck punks
20 that think they own the road. They never use their blinkers.
21 They pass in the right lanes. They turn their music up so
22 loud it shakes my doors when they drive by and they sure
23 don't know how to obey a speed limit. Think it applies to
24 everyone *but* them.
25    And why would they worry about stupid little laws,
26 anyway? They know their dear old mommies and daddies
27 will bail them out of anything they do! *(Mimics.)* "My son
28 wasn't driving drunk, Officer. He always gets like that when
29 he uses too much mouthwash." Or "My little bunny here
30 couldn't have been speeding. She's terrified of going too
31 fast. Your thingy there must be wrong. She would never go
32 that fast."
33    They got an excuse for everything. Heaven forbid a kid
34 should actually have to face the music. Oh no! We can't
35 possibly care about teaching these kids some responsibility.

1    I tell you what, if I could ticket the parents, I would! What
2    are they thinking buying their kids brand new cars before
3    they've ever even worked a day in their bratty little lives?
4    And sports cars at that! The other day, this kid had a
5    Hummer! Do you know how much those things cost?
6         You didn't see things like that in my day. No sir. In my
7    generation, we worked for what we got. Nobody handed us
8    keys to a car, much less a brand new one! I was lucky if I
9    got to *borrow* my parents' car to go to work. Most times I
10   walked. That's right — walked.
11        Just last night I pulled this kid over in a shiny red sports
12   car. I didn't have my equipment on yet so I didn't clock him,
13   but I'm sure he was going seventy at least. Figured I could
14   get him for something else but the punk was clean. Had to
15   let him go. But don't worry, I'll get him the next time!

# It's Definitely Not a Chariot!

(1 Girl, 1 Guy)

1    91. THE PRINCESS'S VERSION
2
3    My mother has always told me that my standards are
4    *way* too high. That I expect *way* too much and that I'm *way*
5    too picky. That's why everyone in my family nicknamed me
6    Princess. I don't care. I do like things a certain way. So
7    what? Is there anything wrong with knowing what you like
8    and what you don't? Of course not.
9    Well, even my mother had to admit my boyfriend's car
10   was sub-standard. It has duct tape in three places and rust
11   spots in more places than I can count! But that's not even
12   the most horrifying part. The thing is a tank. It's the
13   longest, widest car I've ever seen. I think it's from the fifties
14   or something. How it is still running is beyond me. It was his
15   great-grandfather's car. His *great-grandfather's!* Is it even
16   legal to drive a car from like five decades ago? On the
17   highway? The thing plugs along like a turtle on a log. And it
18   sucks up so much gas my boyfriend never has any money
19   to take me on a date. We always have to hang out at my
20   house or go to the park. Well, that's fine every now and then,
21   but I'd like to actually *go* somewhere sometime!
22   But not in that *contraption!* I would die if my friends saw
23   me riding around in that. I would probably die anyway
24   because the thing is a death trap! No air bags, no anti-lock
25   brakes! It barely has seatbelts. Oh, and it definitely does *not*
26   have air conditioning. No wonder. I doubt the car could run
27   the engine and the a-c at the same time. What kind of a car
28   doesn't have air conditioning? It gets to a hundred degrees

1 around here.

2 So, maybe I do have high standards because if he
3 doesn't get rid of that silver tank soon, this princess is
4 finding another prince!

5

6 92. THE PRINCE'S VERSION

7

8 I have the coolest car. Not your average sporty blow-the-
9 stripes-off-the-highway kind of cool car. But a big-as-a-tank,
10 can-destroy-stuff-and-not-even-know-it kind of cool car. The
11 thing is indestructible! I've hit more curbs, mailboxes, road
12 signs, and road trash than I can count. Not because I'm a
13 bad driver, but because I *can!* This car is *solid!* Nothing
14 plastic or fiberglass. Sure, it dents a little, but that's the
15 beauty of it.

16 But the real beauty is I got it totally for free. It used to
17 be my great-grandfather's and when he died, he left it for
18 me. He got it new and treated that thing like a baby. Oil
19 changes, tune-ups. Anything the car needed, he did it. Or
20 rather, he and I would do it. He showed me everything I
21 needed to know. We spent so many Sundays huddled under
22 the hood of that car. Every time I drive, I think about those
23 times. I would give anything to have another Sunday being
24 a grease monkey with my great-grandfather.

25 Of course it bugs my girlfriend that I drive it. She turns
26 her nose up, but only because she refuses to see the quality
27 of the car. Just because it doesn't look all shiny and new
28 she thinks it's a piece of trash. Trash! The car's a gem! An
29 antique even! How can anyone not see how great it is?

30 Sure, it guzzles a little more gas than most cars. But
31 certainly no more than some of the SUVs they have now.
32 And this car has durability! Who knows how long it's going
33 to last? I may be able to pass it down to my son one day.
34 Wouldn't that be awesome? The car is so old it'll look
35 futuristic by then. My kid would be the talk of his school.

1    Kind of like me. Well, let them talk! I'll put my car up against
2    theirs any day of the week. Not to race, of course, but for
3    demolition! I'd make minced meat of them.

# Crash Test Dummy

(1 Guy, 1 Girl)

93. MATTHEW'S VERSION

It seemed like a good idea. The better of the two options. I was tired. She wasn't. So why wouldn't I let her drive? *(Pause)* Because *obviously* she *can't* drive! What was I thinking? Letting Amber get in the driver's seat of my car! It was only two blocks. Two! Who wrecks a car in two blocks?

Now my insurance is doubling and my parents have grounded me for four months. *(Mimics.)* "You knew the rules about no one driving your car." Well, excuse me for thinking it was better to let her drive than for me to drive half-asleep. Of course I woke up pretty fast when that car slammed into us. Not his fault, though. Amber completely ran the stop sign. Says she didn't even see it. How do you *not see* a big red sign with big white letters that says *s-t-o-p!*

It's so unfair. Why shouldn't her insurance pay to fix that guy's car? She was the one driving. And how do you possibly cause so much damage to a vehicle when you're doing *less than thirty miles an hour,* anyway? What was the car made of, plastic? Papier-mâché? The thing crumpled like a dry leaf. Thank goodness no one was hurt or I'd probably never be able to get insurance again. And of course I couldn't afford collision insurance on my car, so I can't even get the dent fixed.

You'd think she'd at least offer to pay for that. But why bother? She hasn't got a dime to her name. It'd just be empty promises. No. I'm stuck with it. My car looks like a

1 junker. But it doesn't really matter since I'm not allowed to
2 drive again for months. To be honest, I think my parents
3 were just looking for an excuse to ground me. They're way
4 too uptight about the whole driving thing. Keep quoting
5 statistics about teenage driving issues. Well, I guess Amber
6 just helped prove their point. Just one more thing I can
7 thank her for. If I didn't love her so much, I would never
8 speak to her again!
9
10                              94. AMBER'S VERSION
11
12      I'll be lucky if my boyfriend ever speaks to me again.
13 This is the worst thing a girl can do. Worse than cheating
14 even. I wrecked his car! His previously non-dented, not even
15 a little bit dinged car! And now the whole right side is caved
16 in ... because of me!
17      I didn't even see the stop sign. I was too worried about
18 driving his car. Making sure I wasn't going to hit the curb or
19 anything. Why would he put me under that kind of
20 pressure?! He should've known better than to let me drive.
21 I *know* how completely protective and insane he is about
22 that thing. How did he think I would be able to relax and
23 actually drive it?
24      *(Pause)* Not that it's his fault. Really. I'm not trying to
25 blame him or anything. Especially since he's being so nice
26 about it all. He didn't even yell at me when it happened. He
27 was more worried about me than his car. I couldn't believe
28 it! He was so sweet. I never dreamed he cared more about
29 me than his precious car. But how long can that last?
30 Reality is going to sink in and he's going to get mad, right?
31 Realize that because of *me* his perfectly bodied car now
32 looks like a piece of junk.
33      I don't know what to do. How to make things better. I'd
34 offer to pay to fix the damages, but I can't even imagine how
35 much stuff like that costs. I barely have twenty dollars from

1   baby-sitting. I sure don't have thousands! And I can't tell
2   my parents about it. They'd kill me for driving — and
3   wrecking! — someone else's car.
4       Somehow I'll make it up to him. Help him with his
5   homework or do his chores for months. *(Pause)* **Only now**
6   he's avoiding me. Saying he's grounded for months. How
7   can *he* be grounded? It wasn't even his fault!

# They're Not Mine!

## (2 Girls)

1                    95. MADISON'S VERSION

2

3     OK, so I know it's lame. Worse than the whole my-dog-
4 ate-my-homework story. In fact, that's probably more
5 believable than this. Which is why my parents are totally
6 freaking out. I can hear them downstairs yelling. They don't
7 even know what to do with me. I've never been grounded in
8 my life. They're completely clueless on how to do it. Or what
9 to ground me from.

10     Come on! Doesn't that tell them something? My record
11 is so clean, I could apply for President one day and even the
12 FBI or the CIA wouldn't be able to find dirt on me.

13     So how can they not believe what I'm telling them? Even
14 if it is the most cliché reason around? Haven't they ever
15 learned that things aren't always as they appear? Don't
16 judge a book by its cover and all that jazz?

17     I know it was a stupid thing to do. I *know* if someone
18 else had found them, like a teacher or the principal, or
19 worse, the coach, my reputation would be ruined. I could
20 have a black mark on my otherwise glowing school record. I
21 could possibly kiss an athletic scholarship good-bye! I *know*
22 all of this! But *not thinking* was my only mistake. Why won't
23 anyone believe me?

24     *(Yelling down the stairs to parents)* They are *not* my
25 cigarettes! I was holding them for a friend! And yes, I know
26 that's what everyone says! But this time it's the truth!

## 96. MOTHER'S VERSION

You think you know your kid. Think you know what they would and wouldn't do. And then something like this happens. Something you pray will never happen. You worry your whole parental life and you think you're almost home free — I mean, graduation is less than a year away! And then your daughter, your normally sane and perfect daughter, practically throws it all away! And for what? To look cool with her friends? To fit in? To impress some guy? To get lung cancer?

Does she know how much trouble she would've gotten into? Does she even remember what the coach said she would do if she found out one of the girls on the team was smoking? Kick her off the team! *Off the team!* All these years of practice. All those special sessions. All our hopes for a scholarship. Down the drain! Good-bye, college scouts! Good-bye, free money! And then what? Work fast food for the rest of her life? Chain smoking on her breaks?

How could she do this? Be so irresponsible? So *stupid?* *(Pacing)* What do I do? What do other parents do? I've never had to do this before. What works the best? What do I even ground her from? What about the whole making her *eat* the cigarettes? I've heard people do that. Would it hurt her? Would it help? Would it stop this need to puff vile chemicals into her body?

I'm so mad I can't even think straight! But I'm thinking enough to not believe that load of bull she's trying to shovel at me! *(Mimics.)* "They're not mine!" Does she think I was born yesterday? Kids have been using that excuse since they invented cigarettes! In fact, I used that line on my own parents.

# I See Dead People

(2 Guys)

1        97. ELI'S VERSION

2

3        I see dead people. And it is *so* cool! The most amazing
4    part is we get to touch them. We can poke around in them,
5    lift out their organs, and everything. It's the most awesome
6    thing I've ever done. I thought this whole two-week summer
7    medical program would be lame-o. A lot of money for a
8    whole lot of nothing. Boy was I wrong! They don't care we're
9    only high school students. They're treating us like future
10   doctors! Funny thing is half these kids only came because
11   they wanted a trip to Phoenix. I bet they're regretting *that*
12   now!
13       Not me. I wish I'd known about this last year. Look at
14   me! I'm holding someone's heart in my hand. Not too many
15   people can say something like that. And now I finally
16   understand what they mean by "dead weight." This arm
17   weighs a ton. And it's cold, too. And hard. Not squishy and
18   soft like when you're alive. It's like touching a mannequin.
19   The smell's not so bad either, once you get used to it. I was
20   kind of hoping for a little of that rotting flesh kind of thing
21   so I'd get to see what that smells like. You see people gag
22   in the movies all the time over it. I'm curious as to how bad
23   it can actually be. But they've pumped these things full of
24   formaldehyde or something because they only smell like
25   chemicals, not like month-old corpses.
26       I tell you what. I might just have to change from wanting
27   to be a surgeon to being a mortician, because this is the
28   coolest thing I've ever seen!

1    98. STUART'S VERSION
2
3    I see dead people. And it is so *not* cool! This is the most
4 disgusting thing I've ever seen in my life. And they want us
5 to touch them! No, they don't *want* us to touch them, they
6 *expect* us to touch them. Like we're some kind of freaks or
7 something. I don't want to touch dead bodies. I want to be
8 a doctor! I expect that all of my patients are going to be
9 alive, not dead. *(Pause)* Otherwise, who's going to pay their
10 bill? Who's going to pay for my summer home and silver
11 convertible Porsche?
12    OK, kidding aside. I did not sign up to touch cold, rock-
13 hard bodies that have been sitting here like frozen people
14 popsicles for who knows how long. It's gross. And it's
15 probably very unsanitary. Who knows what these people
16 died of? Do I really want to put my hands into someone's
17 dead body? I might catch something!
18    Don't they know we're just a bunch of high schoolers?
19 I've still got time to change my mind. Maybe I'll be an
20 engineer or something. Isn't it a little too soon to be
21 subjecting me to rotting corpses? I thought we would tour
22 a hospital. Maybe shadow a couple of different kinds of
23 doctors. Hey, I'd even be up for seeing a baby born or
24 something. Maybe I could even stomach watching a minor
25 operation. But you've got to build to something like this!
26 You can't just throw us into a morgue and expect us not to
27 vomit our guts out. *(Pause)* Speaking of guts ... *(Gag)* what
28 is *that?* Oh my gosh, I think that guy over there just pulled
29 out someone's intestine!
30    Get me out of here. I'm going to be sick!

# French Kisser

(1 Girl, 1 Guy)

1                          **99. PAIGE'S VERSION**

2

3       I think there's something wrong with me. In fact, I *know*
4    there is. All my friends think I've lost my mind. How can
5    they possibly understand when I can't even understand it
6    myself?
7       I mean I totally love my boyfriend. We get along great.
8    We like the same things and we always have a blast together
9    ... until we're alone. Which is why I avoid it at all costs. Then
10   he thinks I'm mad at him. But he gets all cuddly and wants
11   to kiss me and here's the weird part: I can't stand the whole
12   kissing thing. When his lips come at me, I just want to
13   vomit! It's not him, either. At least I don't think he's doing
14   anything wrong. And he's always really good about having
15   fresh breath. Probably because he's paranoid that I never
16   want to kiss him!
17      So what's wrong with me? I'm your normal teenage girl
18   in every other way. Why can't I get past this? It's just the
19   feel of it ... the texture ... you know, it's like my friend Ellie
20   who can't eat Jell-O because the slippery-slimy feeling
21   totally grosses her out. I've seen her gag trying to eat it. But
22   I love Jell-O! So why can't I kiss Caleb?
23      I don't know what I'm going to do. I can only go on so
24   many kiss-free days before he figures out something is
25   seriously wrong. Maybe I just need to desensitize myself
26   somehow. *(Pause)* I know! I won't eat anything but Jell-O for
27   this whole week. Then by the weekend, I'll be ready!

1    ## 100. CALEB'S VERSION
2
3    I have bought every kind of mint or mint gum they make.
4  My parents said they're going to buy stock in mouthwash
5  because of me. And yet every time I go to kiss my girlfriend
6  she flinches. Actually, it's more like a grimace. Like when
7  your parents make you eat gross things like asparagus or
8  broccoli.
9    I must be doing something wrong. I've tried fast. I've
10 tried slow. I don't drool. She doesn't seem to like anything
11 I do. That's got to mean something, right? Like maybe she's
12 cheating on me. Kissing some other guy and that's why
13 she's tired of it by the time she sees me.
14   *(Pause)* Or maybe she doesn't really love me like she
15 says. Maybe she's getting ready to break up with me.
16 Probably never wanted to date me in the first place. I had to
17 ask her out three times before she even said yes. All this
18 time she's just been faking having a good time with me.
19 Biding her time until she found someone else!
20   I should've known. I'm such an idiot. She doesn't even
21 like me! Why would she? Look at her! She's totally hott! She
22 could date anyone in the school ... why would she pick me?
23   Obviously, I can't even kiss right! *(Walks off disgusted.)*

# Overprotective Dad

(1 Girl, 1 Guy))

101. SHELBY'S VERSION
2

3      My dad thinks he's *so* funny! He's probably still laughing
4  over last night. It wasn't even the least bit funny. Look at
5  me. Do I look like I'm laughing? No!
6      He actually met my boyfriend at the door with his
7  hunting rifle! I'm not kidding. You should've seen Gary's
8  face. I wouldn't have been surprised if he'd peed his pants
9  right then and there. His face went totally white. He tried to
10 joke it off, but you could tell he was completely
11 uncomfortable. And Dad didn't help any. He kept a straight
12 face the whole time, and he kept interrogating him. Like the
13 guy was some kind of serial killer or something! I'm
14 surprised he didn't fingerprint him or put him through a lie
15 detector.
16     I kept telling Gary that Dad was just a kidder. That he
17 was pulling his leg, but I could tell he didn't believe me. Why
18 would he? My dad had a gun pointed at him! We couldn't get
19 out of there fast enough.
20     I figured we would forget the whole thing and have a
21 great time. I mean, come on, it was a *little* bit funny when
22 you think about it. But Gary could not relax. He was so
23 uptight and worried about making my dad mad that he
24 brought me home by eight o'clock. Eight o'clock! Four hours
25 *before* my curfew. We didn't even see the movie we planned
26 on. And because a nice restaurant would take too long, he
27 brought me to a fast food burger joint!
28     Next time I have a date, I'm meeting him there. No way

1 am I bringing another guy home to my dad, the wannabe
2 comedian!
3
4 102. GARY'S VERSION
5
6    I waited two years to ask this girl Shelby out. Took me
7 that long to get up my nerve. She's so pretty and popular, I
8 never thought she'd say yes. Well, now I know why! No other
9 guy would be stupid enough to date her. Oh, it's not her
10 that's the problem. It's her psycho father. He's like
11 something out of a horror movie. Last night, when I went to
12 pick Shelby up, he met me at the door with a rifle. A real
13 shoots-bullets-and-kills-things rifle!
14    You think I would've turned and ran, but no! I'm stupid
15 enough to go on in. The guy questioned me for about half an
16 hour.
17    "Where are you taking my daughter?"
18    "Dinner and the movies."
19    "What time do you plan on bringing her back?"
20    "What time does she have to be home, sir?"
21    "Do you drink?"
22    "No. I'm underage, sir."
23    "Do you smoke?"
24    "No. I tried it once. It made me sick."
25    "What would your last girlfriend say about you if I called
26 her?"
27    What could I possibly say to that? She'd probably say all
28 kinds of bad things — that's why she's my *ex*-girlfriend. I
29 shrug and say, "I don't know." So you know what he does?
30 Pulls out a phone book and starts looking up her number.
31 I'm not kidding. If Shelby hadn't stopped him, he would've
32 called Abby and grilled her about me. Who knows what
33 would've happened then!
34    I don't even know why he was so uptight. It's not like I'm
35 a jock or a player or anything. I've only had a couple of

1  girlfriends. And look at me — no tattoos or funky piercings.
2  My hair's decent. I'm not wearing any chains or anything.
3  Why did he treat me like one of America's Most Wanted?
4      The worst part is, I had a blast with Shelby ... for the few
5  short hours we were together. I really think we connected.
6  But there's no way I'm going anywhere near that girl again.
7  Ever! At least not until they've locked up her crazy old man.

# About the Author

This is Rebecca Young's fifth book for teens. Regarding her inspiration for the 400 plus monologues so far, she says, "When you raise three girls, it's all about comedy and tragedy. And a whole realm of emotions in between." Friends and family (she won't dare say who), television, and just a plain old overactive imagination help Rebecca create a wide array of monologues to choose from.

For many years, Rebecca wrote and directed drama for middle and high school students for her church. She co-founded a group called One Voice. It was a dream of hers to combine writing, acting, and helping youth.

Rebecca currently works in a totally "non-dramatic" profession as a technical trainer in Lexington, Kentucky. She has a BA in Communications/Marketing from the University of Kentucky.

Ms. Young lives with her husband Frank, three wonderful and dramatic daughters (Heather, Kristina, and Ashley), and a cat, who is now called Expensive Kitty since he broke his leg and cost almost a house payment to fix — but is worth every penny!

Whether you are an actor or a writer, she suggests this anonymous quote as a daily mantra: "You aren't finished when you lose; you are finished when you quit."

Never give up hope.

# Order Form

**Meriwether Publishing Ltd.**
PO Box 7710
Colorado Springs, CO 80933-7710
Phone: 800-937-5297  Fax: 719-594-9916
Website: www.meriwether.com

*Please send me the following books:*

_____ **102 Great Monologues  #BK-B315**          $16.95
by Rebecca Young
*A versatile collection of monologues and duologues for student actors*

_____ **Famous Fantasy Character Monologs**          $15.95
**#BK-B286**
by Rebecca Young
*Starring the Not-So-Wicked Witch and more*

_____ **100 Great Monologs  #BK-B276**          $15.95
by Rebecca Young
*A collection of monologs, duologs and triologs for actors*

_____ **Winning Monologs for Young Actors**          $15.95
**#BK-B127**
by Peg Kehret
*Honest-to-life monologs for young actors*

_____ **Encore! More Winning Monologs for**          $15.95
**Young Actors  #BK-B144**
by Peg Kehret
*More honest-to-life monologs for young actors*

_____ **The Flip Side  #BK-B221**          $15.95
by Heather H. Henderson
*64 point-of-view monologs for teens*

_____ **Young Women's Monologs from**          $15.95
**Contemporary Plays  #BK-B272**
edited by Gerald Lee Ratliff
*Professional auditions for aspiring actresses*

**These and other fine Meriwether Publishing books are available at
your local bookstore or direct from the publisher. Prices subject to
change without notice. Check our website or call for current prices.**

Name: _____ email:_____

Organization name: _____

Address: _____

City: _____ State: _____

Zip: _____ Phone: _____

❏  **Check enclosed**

❏  **Visa / MasterCard / Discover / Am. Express #** _____

Signature: _____  Expiration date: _____ / _____
      *(required for credit card orders)*

**Colorado residents:** Please add 3% sales tax.
**Shipping:** Include $3.95 for the first book and 75¢ for each additional book ordered.

❏  *Please send me a copy of your complete catalog of books and plays.*

# Order Form

**Meriwether Publishing Ltd.**
PO Box 7710
Colorado Springs, CO 80933-7710
Phone: 800-937-5297  Fax: 719-594-9916
Website: www.meriwether.com

*Please send me the following books:*

_____ **102 Great Monologues  #BK-B315**   **$16.95**
by Rebecca Young
*A versatile collection of monologues and duologues for student actors*

_____ **Famous Fantasy Character Monologs**   **$15.95**
**#BK-B286**
by Rebecca Young
*Starring the Not-So-Wicked Witch and more*

_____ **100 Great Monologs  #BK-B276**   **$15.95**
by Rebecca Young
*A collection of monologs, duologs and triologs for actors*

_____ **Winning Monologs for Young Actors**   **$15.95**
**#BK-B127**
by Peg Kehret
*Honest-to-life monologs for young actors*

_____ **Encore! More Winning Monologs for**   **$15.95**
**Young Actors  #BK-B144**
by Peg Kehret
*More honest-to-life monologs for young actors*

_____ **The Flip Side  #BK-B221**   **$15.95**
by Heather H. Henderson
*64 point-of-view monologs for teens*

_____ **Young Women's Monologs from**   **$15.95**
**Contemporary Plays  #BK-B272**
edited by Gerald Lee Ratliff
*Professional auditions for aspiring actresses*

**These and other fine Meriwether Publishing books are available at your local bookstore or direct from the publisher. Prices subject to change without notice. Check our website or call for current prices.**

Name: _____ email:_____

Organization name: _____

Address: _____

City: _____ State: _____

Zip: _____ Phone: _____

❑ **Check enclosed**

❑ **Visa / MasterCard / Discover / Am. Express #** _____

*Signature:* _____
*(required for credit card orders)*

Expiration
date:   _____ / _____

**Colorado residents:** Please add 3% sales tax.
**Shipping:** Include $3.95 for the first book and 75¢ for each additional book ordered.

❑ *Please send me a copy of your complete catalog of books and plays.*